TECHNOLOGIES
OF SEEING

FROM THE LIBRARY OF

GARY METZ

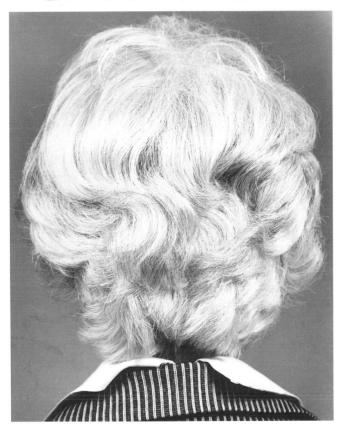

A 1972 GRADUATE OF VISUAL STUDIES WORKSHOP, GARY METZ WAS
AN ACCOMPLISHED PHOTOGRAPHER AND NOTABLE SCHOLAR.

OCTOBER 14, 1941 – SEPTEMBER 28, 2010

TECHNOLOGIES
OF SEEING

Photography, Cinematography and Television

Brian Winston

BRITISH FILM INSTITUTE

bfi

BFI PUBLISHING

First published in 1996 by the
British Film Institute
21 Stephen Street
London W1P 2LN

The British Film Institute exists to promote appreciation, enjoyment, protection
and development of moving image culture in and throughout the whole of the
United Kingdom. Its activities include the National Film and Television Archive;
the National Film Theatre; the Museum of the Moving Image; the London Film
Festival; the production and distribution of film and video; funding and support for
regional activities; Library and Information Services; Stills, Posters and Designs;
Research; Publishing and Education and the monthly *Sight and Sound* magazine.

British Library Cataloguing-in-Publication Data
A catalogue record for this book is available from the British Library

ISBN   0-85170-601–0
         0-85170-602–9 pbk

Cover design and photography by Nick Livesey

Typesetting by D R Bungay Associates, Burghfield, Berks.

Printed in Great Britain by
St Edmundsbury Press Ltd, Bury St Edmunds, Suffolk

Contents

For Adèle, Jessica & Aekold Helbrass
&
the dog Pym

Preface

This series of essays follows up a more general study of the histories of tele-communications technologies published in 1986 (*Misunderstanding Media*, London: Routledge and Kegan Paul; Cambridge, Mass.: Harvard University Press). Although I dealt in that book with the development of television and the first phase of holography, I did not touch upon the technology of film. These present essays seek to make good that lacuna and to bring the television and holographic story into the age of high-definition TV (assuming we are in any such 'age', that is).

Some of this material has been published in earlier versions. The model proposed for technological change, here somewhat revised, appears first in *Misunderstanding Media*. An introductory version of some elements of the history of the technology of film in chapter one is offered in 'How Are Media Born and Developed' in John Downing, Ali Mohammadi and Annabelle Sreberny-Mohammadi (eds), *Questioning the Media: A Critical Introduction*, (Thousand Oaks: Sage, 1995). Chapter two is based on an article, 'A Whole Technology of Dyeing: A Note on Ideology and the Apparatus of the Chromatic Moving Image', *Dædalus*, vol. 114 no. 4, Fall 1985. The account of 16mm in chapter three has never been published. A somewhat less technologised version of chapter four first appeared as 'HDTV in Hollywood: Lights, Camera, Inaction', *Gannett Center Journal*, Columbia University, NY, Summer 1989. (This shorter version was reprinted in: Everette Dennis and John Pavlik (eds), *Demystifying Media Technology*, Mountain View, Calif.: Mayfield Publishing, 1989.) Chapter five refers to a brief history of holography in *Misunderstanding Media* but is otherwise wholly new.

I owe thanks, therefore, to two editors apart from those named above: Stephen Graubard of *Dædalus* and Huntington Williams III, then editor of the *Gannett Center Journal*. And in addition, I have received valued comments from Charles Musser (who guessed), Roberta Pearson and Paul Walton. The translation on p. 120 is by Eugene Stemp. Finally, my thanks to the BFI – to Colin MacCabe for agreeing to this idea and to Ed Buscombe for editing, help and general all-round support; and to my best 'extra reader'.

Introduction: Necessities and Constraints

A Pattern of Technological Change

This book is concerned with one basic question: How does technological change occur in mass communications? My starting point is to deny the obvious answer that technological change occurs as a result of the workings of the collective creative mind of technologists; that technologies in communications (and, indeed, everywhere else) are primarily the products of unfettered human creativity. Instead the book adopts a model for such change which suggests that social needs of various sorts govern the technological agenda in this area, conditioning the creativity of technologists so that on the one hand developments are pushed, while on the other their potential for social disruption is constrained.

On Technological Determinism

Fernand Braudel puts it thus:

> First the accelerator, then the brake: the history of technology seems to consist of both processes, sometimes in quick succession: it propels human life onward, gradually reaches new forms of equilibrium on higher levels than in the past, only to remain there for a long time, since technology often stagnates, or advances only imperceptibly between one 'revolution' or innovation and another.[1]

The crucial question, however, is: who is the driver here? Within the dominant framework of the idea of progress, the commonly held assumption is that it is the technologist who has control of the pedals. This view does not imply approval. There are those (the ecologically minded, for example) who might say the technologist drives badly. The more extreme might say that the technologist has fallen asleep at the wheel. But whatever our opinion of the driver, there is a clear understanding that, happy or alarmed, the rest of us are all passengers and, therefore, more or less powerless.

This position can be termed 'technological determinism'. Technological determinism, as Raymond Williams explained,

> is an immensely powerful and now largely orthodox view of the nature of social change. New technologies are discovered by an essentially internal process of research and development, which then sets the conditions of social change and progress. Progress, in particular, is the history of these inventions, which 'created the modern world'. The effects of the

1

technologies whether direct or indirect, foreseen or unforeseen, are as it were the rest of history.[2]

The technological determinist vision is important not simply as a powerful and somewhat unexamined explanation of the world in which we live. It also intervenes directly in that world at the level of political policy-making and thereby impacts on all our lives. Politicians of all persuasions profess a belief in it. It allows them, elegantly, to disguise their own agendas; to pretend that they are in the grip of forces both elemental and unnatural. Man-made the forces might be, but they are not of the politicians' making. Thus, when a politician, in this random example the late President of France François Mitterand, says 'Science and technology are going to develop forcing humans to conceive of a different society',[3] he appears to be as much in the grip of these forces as the next president.

And so are captains of industry such as Rupert Murdoch. His search for world multi-media domination has nothing to do with the logics of capitalism, much less personal ambition. On the contrary, as one British socialist politician put it: 'Technological changes are *driving* different sectors of the industry – newspapers, television, telephony, video, computers, cable and satellite – closer together' (emphasis added).[4] So what is poor Murdoch to do? He is as much the victim of technology as is President Mitterand or you and I. These examples are chosen absolutely at random and could be endlessly duplicated because technological determinism is a truth universally acknowledged. It suffuses the computer/technology and editorial pages of the quality press as much as it permeates the corridors of political and business power.

But, despite its pervasiveness, it seems to me clearly absurd to suggest that technological determinism renders Mitterand and Murdoch powerless (for all that it indisputably works to convince the rest of us that our self-evident powerlessness is inevitable, unavoidable and without human agency). 'The basic assumption of technological determinism', wrote Williams, 'is that a new technology – a printing press or a communications satellite – "emerges" from technical study and experiment. It then changes the society or the sector into which it has "emerged". "We" adapt to it, because it is the new modern way.'[5] To dispute that this is indeed what happens is heretical, self-evidently absurd. The devices tumble out of the laboratory, the products of untrammelled human creativity, and they change our world. Denying the technological determinist vision runs not only against the grain of the times but also the risk of being dismissed as luddite.[6] Nevertheless I wish to do this. I wish to suggest that such an obvious understanding is wrong. Holding a technological determinist view is, I would claim, like believing that it is the movement of the leaves on the trees which creates the wind.[7]

Let us take an opposing position, one which proposes that the technologist is – if not merely a passenger – then no more than the mechanic servicing a vehicle designed and built to society's specification. We, collectively, are in the driver's seat. This is certainly Braudel's view: although science and technology, as they are commonly understood, are 'uniting today to dominate the world – such unity *depends necessarily* upon the role played by present-day societies, which may encourage or restrain progress, today as in the past' (emphasis added).[8] In other words, in the dance of history society always leads technology.

The science and technology that produced the set of phenomena known as the industrial revolution were all to hand centuries before they were actually applied to achieve that effect. It was the socio-economic configurations of Britain in the 18th century that accelerated the application of the technologies involved, just as the socio-economic conditions in, say, southern Germany or northern Italy two centuries earlier put a brake on the same applications of those identical technologies. In a narrow sense, technological development is always as Braudel says it was of the industrial revolution: 'Innovations were quite clearly dependent on the state of the market: they were introduced only when they met persistent demand from consumers.'[9]

I want to argue that this sort of historical pattern holds true for current (and, almost certainly, short-term future) innovations – at least in the field of communications. To do this we need first to go beyond 'the market' which is but a subset of the social. As Braudel himself warns, economics are no better, by themselves, at explaining these phenomena than is technology. He is not suggesting substituting economics as an alternative monocausal explanation for change (*pace* a vulgar Marxism) because all monocausal explanations are inadequate. Rather, he demonstrates the need for complex, 'thick' explanations. Second, this insight into the primacy of society as the main agent in setting technology's agenda applies more widely than just to what we might see as the more overtly social deployments of technological developments, such as the industrial revolution. What is less clearly perceived is that the sort of prefiguration Braudel points to in the industrial revolution occurs (indeed, necessarily occurs) with all innovations great and small. The state of the market, or better, of society is the crucial factor in enabling the development and diffusion of any communications technology or in hindering it. That is as true of the computer chip and the Internet as it was of the telegraph and the telephone. Thus, innovations are the creatures of society in a general sense.

Again let me stress that I am only concerned with *communications* technologies. That is to say, this claim is without prejudice to what might or might not be the case in other fields. With these communications technologies, though, I observe a sequence of events with a more or less regular pattern which allows me to propose a model to describe the underlying nature of their introduction and diffusion over the past two centuries and more. The pattern displayed by the model is perforce quite complicated since it needs to take account of the uneven nature of the phenomenon – the accelerators as well as the brakes. It also needs to absorb Williams's fundamental insight as to the primacy of the social sphere.

Modelling Technological Change
The pattern is, first and foremost, historic; that is, in Saussurean terms, diachronic. But, just as Saussurean linguistics has both a diachronic and

3

synchronic dimension, so too, it seems to me, does the pattern of technological change in communications. At any given discrete moment the situation of a technology can be represented by the synchronic intersection of three fields: science, in its original sense of fundamental knowledge (which might or might not encompass theoretical concepts); technology – the application of such knowledge 'in the metal' (as the engineers say, when actually meaning in any material, of course); and, encompassing and framing all, society.

A good way to think about how these three intersect is offered by carrying the analogy of the Saussurean model further. Just as utterance, in Saussurean linguistics, is a surface expression of deep-seated mental competence, so too can technology be thought of as a species of 'utterances' in a 'language' called science. Utterance is the surface expression of the deeper structure and, therefore, stands in a structural relationship to language. Chomsky's terms, 'performance' for 'utterance' and 'competence' for 'language', make this clearer. Technology is a performance of a competence arising from science (or knowledge). Technology stands in a structural relationship to science.

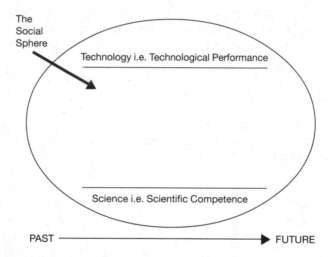

The Social Sphere

Technology i.e. Technological Performance

Science i.e. Scientific Competence

PAST ⟶ FUTURE

In the original linguistic model, the transformation from mental competence to physical performance is rule-governed. In this analogous application, the structural relationship between scientific competence and technological performance can still be thought of as a transformation, but it would be foolish, given the messiness of the social sphere in which a myriad of factors are in play, to describe it as rule-governed. I would want to split the difference between a strict rule-governed relationship (in linguistics, a grammar) and a totally random relationship. The pattern is too regular to be random but not so regular as to be completely predictive.

A technology moves from inchoate scientific knowledge (which itself is conditioned by society) to wide diffusion in society via a number of transformations. The first and most obvious is the business of translating scientific understanding into a device that exists in the world. This requires a

4

transformation in the mind of the technologists who are, remember, themselves the products, and indeed the prisoners, of their cultures.

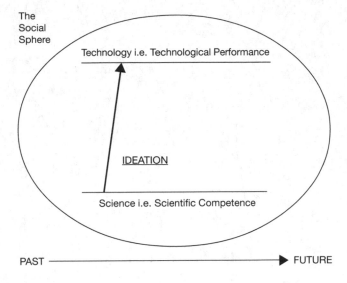

Crudely, this is the idea of the device – and in the model we can describe this as a transformation termed 'ideation'. This work of 'ideation' produces the technological performances we call prototypes.

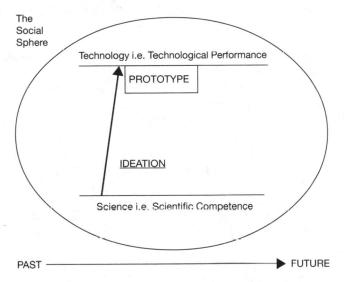

What then transforms the prototype into the invention? We are here dealing with Braudel's observation that technologies can remain unexploited for long periods of time. They languish, as it were, in the prototype phase, conceived and produced because the technologist, as a social being, sees a possibility of a use but the rest of society does not. Braudel's accelerator is not activated. In this model, acceleration can be thought of as an external social force, or combination of such forces, acting on the production of prototypes. When these forces come into play, they transform the prototype.

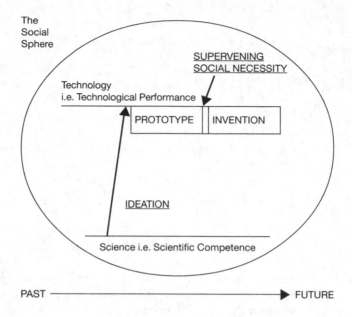

In effect, these accelerating social forces can be described as supervening social necessity, transforming prototype into an invention and enabling its diffusion.

This introduction of supervening social necessity explains the phenomenon of simultaneous 'invention'. Obviously, if technologists are working to an agenda determined by society and subject to further social forces such as their own conditioning, they are not as likely (as popular accounts suggest) to make 'eureka' discoveries. They are, as the historical record demonstrates, more likely to find similar or identical solutions for the same social need and to do so more or less at the same time. (This is literally true, for example, of the telephone. Alexander Graham Bell and his rival Elisha Gray both arrived at the Washington patent office on the same February day in 1876 with designs for such a thing.)

It is also the case that the difference between prototype and invention is more complex than is usually assumed to be the case. It is not, for example, always true that the invention works better and that the prototype or prototypes work less well. For instance, patents existed for the use of magnetic tape as a memory or storage medium for calculators from 1943. But, almost certainly because these were German (indeed, 'Nazi'), the earliest diffused computer memory systems were based on glass tubes filled with mercury, cathode ray tubes or nickel or iron-oxide plated metal drums.[10] The stated reasons for avoiding tape included, for example, the dirt problem; but this would be solved within another five years by nothing more complex than a dust-free cabinet housing for the tape deck.[11]

Further, it could be that on occasion neither prototype nor invention works very well. Again, the telephone is a case in point. Bell was legally awarded the patent but Gray's device was closer to solving the problem of 'the electric speaking telephone'. In effect, neither was to be diffused. The telephone technology that was actually to work in the world was created in an intense research and development phase involving these two, Watson, Edison, Berliner and others over the next three years to 1879.[12] Further examples to prove these points are laid out, as are descriptions of different classes of prototypes, inventions and supervening social necessities in *Misunderstanding Media.*[13]

New technologies contain considerable disruptive power. Many believe that this power is exercised in an untrammelled way and that our world is utterly transformed by these technologies. But what is transformed? Our economic system is, fundamentally, unchanged by these devices. Indeed they are the creatures and products of that system. Our political structures remain largely recognisable as does our cultural life and, despite hyperbolic discourse that claims otherwise, our sense of ourselves. It all depends on where you stand. For a technological determinist, whether of conservative or radical bent, the impact of the technology looms large and the changes wrought are great. The potential changes (which are always apparently to occur within the next five years to ten years) are greater yet, quite often wholly transformative.

But I would take a different view. I still see, after two centuries (at least) of these supposedly transformative technologies impacting on our world, patriarchy, capitalism, nations (and tribes), the Queen, the Stars and Stripes, wars of religion, exploitation of labour, leisure versus work and so on. So, for example, what interests the technological determinist is that the American radical right endlessly exploits the Internet; what interests me is that these folks use the technology to push a social vision two centuries out-of-date. In short, stand close to the technologies and they loom very large; stand away and they blend into the fabric of society. Being digital becomes no big deal.

This is not to argue that new communications technologies (or indeed other areas of technology) have nil effect, occasion no changes. Of course they do. Nor is it to argue that those changes are insignificant. Of course they can be very significant (although even a cursory knowledge of history will very often reduce the scale of change involved.) Rather, it is simply to suggest that these effects and changes are slow to work their way into society. To account for this in the model, the transformation that covers the move of the invention out into the world is conditioned by a social brake not an accelerator. New technologies are constrained and diffused only insofar as their potential for radical disruption is contained or suppressed. That is the brake. The technologies are made to 'fit' into society by this last transformation. This can therefore be termed 'the suppression of radical potential'.

It is the suppression of radical potential which allows the broad continuities of our civilisation to survive the stream of innovations. This suppression is the factor which primarily accounts for Braudel's delays.

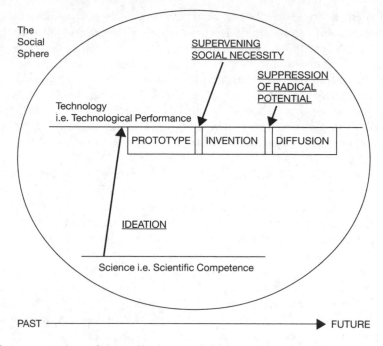

The
Social
Sphere

SUPERVENING
SOCIAL NECESSITY

SUPPRESSION
OF RADICAL
POTENTIAL

Technology
i.e. Technological Performance

| PROTOTYPE | INVENTION | DIFFUSION |

IDEATION

Science i.e. Scientific Competence

PAST ────────────────────────► FUTURE

The suppression of the radical potential of any technology is so well established as to begin to give the appearance of inevitability. So much does diffusion depend on such suppression that, despite the model not being regular enough to produce rule-governed transformations, we can nevertheless think of this transformation as being almost a law – the 'law' of the suppression of radical potential. Television, for instance, was available for full-scale diffusion two decades or so before that actually took place, and not all these lost years can be accounted for by the Second World War. More significant are the complex strategies deployed by the radio and film industries both to control the new medium's effect on their enterprises and to adjudicate their rival ownership claims on it. Again, the complex operation of this transformation and the resultant complexities within the diffusion phase are described more fully in *Misunderstanding Media*.

The purpose of all this is simply to enable us to elucidate the nature of technological progress in communications in a way that meshes with the complexities of these histories. Of necessity, doing this requires rethinking the received accounts of these technological developments in a critical way. The case studies in this book are concerned with image technologies – technologies of seeing, and primarily the technologies of the moving image. I shall take, as the first case, the history of the development of the cinema itself and ask some basic questions: Why did this happen in 1895? Why was film 35mm wide?

Issues of this sort are fundamental to the ways in which we have applied technology to the human act of seeing. These technologies of seeing, and how they are introduced and develop, are the concerns of this book. Why can't colour films photograph black people very easily? Why did 16mm take

8

thirty years to become a professional film stock? Why is high-definition television not available today? How long before we have holographic films and television?

In the chapters that follow each of these questions becomes a case illustrating one or other aspect of the model. Chapter One uses the 'invention' of the cinema to highlight the importance of the social sphere in the history of communications technologies. Chapter Two deals with scientific competence and the ideation transformation – the competencies involved in, and the constraints upon, the technological imagination. Taking the development of colour film stocks, it makes a further argument for the supremacy of the social sphere, on this occasion in determining fundamental research agendas.

Chapter Three explores the nature of the accelerator, that is the importance of supervening social necessities for the development of a technology. The history of 16mm illustrates how the lack of a supervening social necessity limited the diffusion of the technology.

Chapter Four shifts focus to the operation of the brake – the 'law' of the suppression of radical potential. The failure of analogue high-definition television between 1980 and 1995 is not only a good case to demonstrate how the 'law' operates; it also reveals that its power is undiminished in the so-called 'Information Age'.

In the fifth and final chapter, the model is used to offer a necessarily partial answer to another question of delay: where are moving holographic images? This chapter returns, via a consideration of the necessities and constraints in play in the development of this technology, to the basic question: How does technological change occur within the technologies of seeing?

Chapter 1: The Case of the Cinema

The 'Invention' of the Cinema:
Accelerators and Brakes

In What Is Cinema? *André Bazin raises the question of why the cinema was created in 1895 when, technologically speaking, no particular innovation occurred in that year. That is to say, everything the Lumières put together to create a moving image system was already to hand. Most historians are dismissive of this as a problem and either implicitly or explicitly deny that the technology involved was (or could have been) to hand earlier. But this is exactly the sort of question the model proposed in the introduction is designed to help answer. In order to understand how it might do so, however, it is necessary to consider how the history of the birth of the cinema has been treated hitherto.*

Great Men Invent the Cinema

In its simplest form, that is prior to a spate of work beginning in the 1970s on the cinematic apparatus, the dominant received history explained the 'essentially internal process of research and development' on the cinema as nothing more than the chronologically arranged biographies of the scientists and technologists involved in a particular line of inquiry. This sort of account tended to see the development and impact of any technology as an aspect of the progress of great (white) men, women and people of colour or of different cultures not figuring much, if at all.

Such an account of the development of the cinema usually began in 1553 in Italy with della Porta, who refined the dark room, or *camera obscura,* used by astronomers for observation purposes by placing a lens in front of the lens-less pinhole which previously had created the image within the room. Within a century or so, one German monk, Johann Zahn, would shrink this room to the size of a box, the *camera obscura portabilis,* while another, the Jesuit Athanius Kircher, placed a candle within the shrunk box (as it were) and an image drawn on glass between the light source and the lens to create a magic lantern.

So much for lenses and projection; now for movement. Peter Roget, some nineteen years after he began work on his *Thesaurus*, conceived of an explanation (termed 'persistence of vision') as to why the eye can be deceived into thinking a series of slightly different images to be a single moving image. This was in 1824. Device after device, with names like zootrope or thaumatrope, were produced (or 'invented') to animate drawings using the phenomenon of persistence of vision: for example by Paris (English, 1824), Plateau (Belgian, early 1830s), Stampfer (German, 1832).

Next, the principle of persistence of vision must be put together with the idea of projection. In 1852 Captain Franz von Uchatius did this as an aid to his teaching of physics in the Artillery School in Vienna. He animated projected lantern slides of cannon-ball flight. (However, he became Baron von Uchatius because of a subsequent invention in 1879 of the gun metal known as 'Uchatius Steel', the Austrian Empire having its own clear understanding of the relative importance of the two technologies.)

The problem now was how to produce long sequences of minutely variant images. By the time von Uchatius combined the magic lantern with the zootrope, photography was to hand to do this.

That light affected substances was known to everybody who had ever noticed the bleaching properties of sunlight on fabrics. By the first years of the 19th century, investigators such as Thomas Wedgwood, the potter, understood that silver nitrates, conversely, darkened in sunlight. By placing a painting done on glass on top of a piece of leather sensitised with a silver nitrate solution he, in effect, produced a half-tone negative sometime before 1802. (We would call this a photogram because it used light and chemicals to make an image but no camera.) Wedgwood was unable to inspect his result because further exposure to light simply continued the darkening process. He did not know how to 'fix' the image so that, at a given point during its emergence or development, this darkening would stop.

On the other side of the Channel, Nicephore Niépce in 1816 took the idea of photography forward by placing his silver-nitrate sensitised paper against the glass-screen of a very small camera obscura. Although annoyed by the negative results he thereby obtained, he did not appreciate that the answer was to repeat the process in a photogram mode by laying the negative against a second sheet of sensitised material to produce a positive. Why would he? He had not yet discovered how to stop the blackening process and his negative was opaque. His solution was to search through the pharmacopoeia until he found a substance that bleached in light and was 'fixable' – that is, capable of being treated chemically to stop the bleaching process. Such a substance would produce a positive.

He came up with a sort of asphalt – bitumen of Judea. Fixing could be achieved with a mixture of oil of lavender and white petrol. Niépce treated a pewter plate with this bitumen and left it attached to a moderate-sized camera for eight sunny hours one day in the summer of 1826. The image, a view from his window, he then fixed, producing what he called an 'heliograph'. A shy and secretive man, it was not to be Niépce's lot to bring this process before the world. Instead this fell to Louis Daguerre, a showman in the business of exhibiting moving Dioramas, who used cameras of considerable refinement to help him make the huge 70' by 45' paintings he needed for his show. Their mutual lens maker put them in touch with each other.

Niépce died in 1833 and Daguerre continued alone. He returned to the search for a process that used a darkening compound solution based on silver. A copper plate was used as a base. The process he eventually elaborated required considerable chemical treatments, boilings and washings to produce a positive image which was then fixed with a saline solution. In

1839, the patents for 'daguerreotyping', as Daguerre termed his system, were bought by the French nation and given to the world. One immediate problem was that the process was comparatively insensitive to light but within a year or so Peter Voigtländer in Germany had produced a lens sixteen times 'faster' than the one Daguerre used originally and John Godard in London discovered that adding bromines to the process also improved the sensitivity of the plate. An image could be obtain in good light after a mere thirty seconds.

The daguerreotype was not quite photography of course, if you define photography as a system of image making whereby light and chemicals create a negative which can then produce an infinite number of positives. Daguerreotypes were unique positive images – 'as fragile as butterfly's wings', according to one early enthusiast. For all the amazing speed with which daguerreotyping spread across the face of the globe, creating as it went a whole new industry, it was nevertheless a vulnerable technology.

Henry Fox-Talbot, a wealthy English amateur, had produced an alternative process, the Calotype, after pursuing many of the same lines of inquiry as the French during the 1830s. But, crucially, he realised that the second exposure to convert the darkened substance to a positive ought to be on a separate base from the original negative. He also knew how to stop the darkening, to 'fix' the image. In 1841 he patented a process using paper sensitised with silver nitrate. The exposed negative was then developed, fixed, dried and oiled to render it transparent. It was then re-exposed against a second sheet of paper which had been treated with silver chloride. This sheet was then itself developed and fixed. The terms 'photography', 'positive' and 'negative' were all coined by Talbot's friend, the great astronomer Sir John Hershel, to describe the process and elements within it.

Calotypes could not match the exquisite detail of daguerreotypes because of the imperfect transparency of the paper negative; but within a decade, a new negative/positive system was introduced which solved this difficulty. In 1851 Frederick Scott Archer, a British sculptor, took a glass plate which had been washed in collodion – a solution of the explosive substance guncotton in ether, which was originally developed as a dressing for wounds by Christian Schönbein in 1846 in Basle. (Another investigator, Böttger, shadowed Schönbein by developing the same dressing at the same time in Frankfurt.) Scott Archer dipped the glass covered with this gummy transparent wash into a silver nitrate solution. He then exposed the treated plate before the collodion had time to dry and thereby produced transparent negatives every bit as capable of capturing detail as daguerreotypes. He also reduced exposure time to a matter of two or three seconds. He gave the process to the world and died penniless six years later at the age of forty-four.

All this is not quite enough to enable the cinema to be invented. That required a flexible substitute for the glass Uchatius and Scott Archer were using so that sequences of images could be projected rapidly enough for persistence of vision to create the illusion of movement. In 1871 a Dr Richard Leach Maddox suggested in the *British Journal of Photography* that perhaps gelatine might be used instead of collodion.[1] It too was a transparent sticky substance which would cause the silver nitrate to adhere to the glass plate but it could be used in a dry state. In the course of the next decade or so, the application of this possibility allowed a new industry, the commercial manufacturing of dry-plate films, to be established. This advance was the first stage in getting rid of the glass.

During the course of 1884/5, George Eastman, an American bank clerk, produced machinery to put a gelatine emulsion (silver bromide) onto a paper backing which could then be stripped off leaving a transparent negative. He called this film 'Kodak' – in his words a term 'as meaningless as a child's first "goo"'.[2] Previously he too had been making silver-bromide dry-plates on glass, but using paper allowed for the development of a rolled film strip. Four years later, he dispensed with the paper for the emulsion by using instead a transparent celluloid film as the base. Celluloid was a collodion variant which had been patented by one Parkes as a 'transparent support for sensitive coating' in 1856. (Parkes, however, had been unable to make it work.[3]) John Hyatt, an American printer, was able to produce serviceable celluloid sheets in 1869, but he and his brother were primarily interested in the stuff for use (in molded forms) as a substitute for ivory to make, for example, cheap billiard balls or piano keys. It could however also be applied in photography to produce a film base for the light-sensitive silver nitrates. By 1889 this is exactly what Eastman was doing, thereby creating a flexible transparent film strip.

So we now have the projector and the photographic camera and the flexible film as well as a slough of different devices producing the illusion of movement. All that is lacking is the notion that these various elements could be brought together in a system that would project sequences of transparent photographic images. This was not as obvious a connection as it now seems. The real issue of the day was not creating the illusion of movement but rather using the camera as a scientific instrument to stop motion. Investigators, for example the Englishman Eadweard Muybridge who was working in America in the 1870s, produced elaborate photographic apparatuses to solve such age-old conundra as how many feet did a galloping horse have on the ground at any one time. But although Muybridge also built a projection animation device, the zoopraxiscope, he did not use his sequential photographic images in it. Photography was, perhaps, too closely bound up with stop motion.

Muybridge used many cameras for his stop-motion experiments but a French correspondent of his, the physiologist Étienne-Jules Marey, devised a camera that could take twelve images a second on a single glass plate. By 1888 Marey was using flexible paper-backed roll film in this machine. The following year he was using celluloid in his 'photographic rifle'. However, with him too the stop-motion project loomed large and he was even less interested than Muybridge in using his images to re-create a representation of motion.

On Saturday 25 February 1888, Muybridge projected both stop-motion photographs and brief moving sequences of drawings in his zoopraxiscope to an audience in the Music Hall in Orange, New Jersey. On the following

Monday, he visited that community's most famous citizen, Thomas Edison, to propose that the latter's phonograph should be used in synch with the zoopraxiscope.

Nothing came of this suggestion, but Edison did begin to worry about moving pictures. He also met the French pioneer Marey at the Paris Exposition in August of that year and, moreover, bought a Kodak camera from Eastman. Edison then began a series of investigations, with his assistant W. K. L. Dickson, which were to yield, five years later, the first photographic motion-picture device, the Kinetoscope, to be diffused outside the laboratory. But if Muybridge did not think to use photographs, Edison did not think to use projection. His initial model for the movies was an apparatus which somehow matched the basic design of his cylinder phonograph. Instead of the sound-waves caught in wax or tin, this machine would have photographs on a flexible plate wound about the cylinder; and where the loudspeaker horn was in the phonograph an optical viewer would be in this new moving image machine. Even when the principle of projection was introduced into these researches, it was still used to produce a small image that could only be seen by one person at a time, a peep-show, exactly like many of the optical toys which had preceded it. But this, the Kinetoscope, when it finally went forth into the world in 1894, did use sequential photographic images on a strip of flexible celluloid with sprocket holes down the sides to hold it in position. All that remained to 'invent' the cinema was to place such a strip in a mechanised magic lantern.

The Kinetoscope was a considerable success but, perhaps, this in itself led Edison to the belief that projecting the strips would not work. This was despite the fact that a number of researchers and showmen immediately began to think along these lines. In February 1895, two French brothers, Auguste and Louis Lumière, manufacturers of photographic equipment in Lyon, patented a combined motion-picture camera and magic lantern (or projector). It also functioned as a printer. They demonstrated it on 22 March 1895, and on 28 December of the same year, in a basement room in Paris, they projected a number of films made with this device for a paying audience for the first time. They called the machine the Cinématographe and, by this act of naming alone, they therefore have a species of indisputable claim to have 'invented' the cinema.

By this point, of course, the 'invention' of the cinema in a eureka sense of fundamental breakthrough and discovery is impossible. It was really a question of engineering a system out of readily available devices and concepts. This is proved by the fact that by the 1890s there was a rising tide of patents and devices for motion-picture systems, including projected-image systems, of which the Cinématographe is but one. For example, on 1 November 1895, two other brothers, Max and Émile Skladanowsky, unveiled their Bioscope in Berlin. This projected sprocketed film, but the strips lasted only six seconds and the system produced only eight frames per second, requiring the use of two projectors to achieve the illusion of steady movement – albeit with, as can be readily imagined, tremendous flicker. Other devices were of greater significance, notably those produced by

14

a number of Americans which introduced gearing systems within the projector, allowing for each frame of the strip to be held momentarily in the gate before the light source. This intermittent mechanism markedly increased the smoothness of the illusion of movement. Kinetoscope films had been first projected in April 1895 but on a continuous basis. Now C. F. Jenkins and Thomas Arnat at the Cotton States Exposition in Atlanta in September 1895 demonstrated a projector with an intermittent gear. Their advance was exploited by two Kinetoscope dealers, with Edison's blessing, as the Vitascope, even as the Cinématographe was crossing the Atlantic.

This, then, is a history of a steady series of advances beginning in 1553 and culminating 452 years later. A succession of inventive and creative technicians – della Porta, Kircher, Roget, Paris, Plateau, Stampfer, Niépce, Daguerre, Voigtländer, Fox Talbot, Godard, Schönbein, Böttger, Scott Archer, von Uchatius, Parkes and the Hyatts, Maddox, Muybridge, Eastman, Marey, Edison, Dickson, Jenkins and Arnat, the Lumières – march inexorably towards motion pictures. The genius of Italy, Germany, Britain, Austria, Belgium, Switzerland, France and the United States all contribute. Like streams, the magic lantern, the principle of persistence of vision and photography flow together, by the late 19th century, to make the river that is the cinema.

Errors and Omissions

Now it is not that any of the above is actually wrong, or at least, not very wrong. In the first instance, let us just say it is rather incomplete.

To begin again at the beginning: della Porta is credited with putting a lens in the camera obscura but it could well be that it was done earlier since both the room and the lens had been around for centuries. The principle of observing eclipses by looking at the image cast through a pinhole onto the wall of an otherwise dark room, a camera obscura, was known to Arab astronomers by the 9th century at the latest and described by Levi ben Gershon of Arles, who was familiar with the Arabic literature, in a Hebrew book which was translated into Latin in 1342.[4] So who shrank it into a box with a pinhole to make the *camera obscura portablis*? And then who attached a lens to this device?

It is quite possible that a century before della Porta the *camera obscura portabilis* was known in Florence to that brilliant circle of artists and scientists (including Donatello, Ghiberti, Masaccio and Brunelleschi) by whom the first modern European system for effectively representing three-dimensional space on flat surfaces was elaborated by 1435. The work that outlines this perspectival system, *Della pittura* by Leone Battista Alberti, postulates 'a pyramid of sight' having a rectilinear base. This base, which Alberti describes as a 'veil' can also be thought of as a glass upon whose surface the perspectival scene is caught. It comes as no surprise, then, to learn (albeit obscurely enough in the fashion of early Renaissance scientific and magical writing) that Alberti made 'demonstrations' through a tiny opening in a 'little closed box'.[5]

As for the lens, it can be noted that two centuries before that, Roger Bacon, who is credited with the invention of spectacles, had used similar language about light rays on a perpendicular plane. Others are mentioned in the same context. What is indisputable is that an Arab astronomer, Ibn al Haitharn-Alhazan, wrote a book on these matters in the 10th century which was translated into Latin as *De perspectiva* in the 13th century. We can also note that the magic lantern was know to the Chinese possibly as early as 121 BC and certainly by AD 950.[6] It might be as well anyway to put aside Kircher as the 'inventor' of the lantern because although his book *Ars magna lucis et ubrae* (1644) talks of it the illustrations therein are really not accurate. The great seventeeth-century scientist Christian Huyghens, a correspondent of Kircher's, has a better claim. Certainly, the term *'lanterne magique'* is Huyghens's, used to describe a device he had built by 1659 at the latest.[7]

The first and obvious point to note here is the Eurocentric bias of the received account, since it is certainly possible – with transmission from the Chinese to the Arabs and from the Arabs, via the Jews, to the Italians and Germans (or rather to those living in what were to become Italy and Germany) – that these ancient devices and techniques could have been to hand well before the Renaissance. They are not therefore unique to the supposed genius of the West. The second point is that of finding great (or lesser) men, there is little end. But, more importantly, the above received style of history actually involves sequencing of the biographies of 'great men', selecting them on various bases – for instance, in the interest of modern nationalist *amour propre* .

Take persistence of vision. It is Plateau the Belgian who extrapolates the theory of persistence of vision from the phenomenon of retinal after-image retention in his doctoral thesis of 1829. (Actually, in 1829, what was to become Belgium was still part of what was to be the Netherlands. Belgium came into being in 1831.) Nevertheless, if this account were written in French, it would take appropriate note of the francophone Plateau and make other adjustments in emphasis, namely:

On retient généralement de la découverte des frères Lumière qu'elle a permis une représentation de l'image-mouvement. D'autres tentatives l'avaient pourtant précédée sans connaître le même succès; du zootrope de Horner (1834)[8] au kinétoscope de Dickson et Edison (1891), en passant par les expériences de Muybridge sur le zoopraxiscope (1877) et le 'fusil photographique' de Marey (1881). Mais, sur le plan technique, Louis et Auguste Lumière furent les premiers à réussir en 1895 le rencontre du kinétoscope et de la lanterne magique. ... il est nécessaire de remonter encore quelques années en arrière, en 1830, à l'explication physiologique apportée par Joseph Plateau concernant la *persistance rétinienne*. ... La découverte de Plateau annonçait le cinématographe.[9]

However, mine is an account written in English and thus privileges Anglo-American contributions over all others. So what did the Englishmen involved in this element of the enterprise really do?

Roget (who was anyway of Swiss Huguenot stock) was actually concerned with exactly the reverse phenomenon to Plateau (*le physicien belge*). Plateau was interested how the illusion of movement might be created, Roget in how the illusion of statis actually occurs – as when one observes the rotating spokes of a wheel through a vertical slit. Roget had simply noticed this 'optical deception', as he termed it, while idly observing a passing cart through a venetian blind.[10]

But we need to note that the entire concept of persistence of vision is dubious. This came to be the favoured explanation for these phenomena and is still commonly believed and, as we have seen, found in print (and not just in French). However, it has now been discredited, at least in its most basic form, in favour of other more complex descriptions. Persistence of vision has given way to the critical fusion factor. This describes the way in which the retina, because of its inability to keep up with rapid changes in brightness levels, will fail to see, for example, discrete light flashes at rates of more than about thirty flashes a second. Instead, we start to see only a continuous light. Secondly, there is the illusion of apparent movement or phi phenomenon. Here the eye will see two discrete lights mounted a little apart and flashing alternately as one light moving backwards and forwards between the two positions. This too occurs when the flashes become frequent enough.

We now believe that neither of these effects is the result of the image somehow burning itself onto the retina. Instead it arises because of deficiencies in the eye/brain system which fails to respond quickly enough to such changes. However, we still do not have a full understanding of the psychological mechanisms involved but it does seem that we perceive the moving image because we cannot see the gaps (as it were) between the film's frames rather than because the image of one frame lingers (as it were) until the next superimposes itself. To see this failure more positively, one can follow Richard Gregory who suggests that the eye/brain system 'is reasonably tolerant in its demands – which makes the cinema and television economically possible'.[11]

But let us come back to omissions rather than clear errors. Apart from selecting the great men according to one nationalist prejudice or another, there is also a tendency to select on a time basis so that the story unfolds in an even and causally logical way. Biographies are chosen, as it were, to produce narrative drive. The result is that there is often a species of historical amnesia at work. The persistence of vision element also illustrates this tendency.

A Frenchman, d'Arcy, had written a paper for the Academy of Sciences in Paris (which was therefore scarcely obscure) on the same phenomenon as Plateau. He had observed that if one swings a light in a circle swiftly enough it appears to be continuous. But he read this paper in 1765.[12] This means a 'great man' historian would have decades of neglect to explain if d'Arcy is included. It is bad enough that the magic lantern is popular in the 18th century without discovering that more of the elements which go towards cinema were known. If we include d'Arcy, we wreck the little tale of Roget (and Faraday, whom I have, by the way, just left out because he essentially repeated Roget's work in a more sophisticated form) leading to Plateau (which connection Plateau anyway denied) leading to 'wheel of life' optical toys within a matter of years.

Of course, even this narrative drive has its problems. It cannot really begin to explain why nobody puts photographs into these toys despite the fact that

17

both appear around the same time, a point raised by André Bazin.[13] It was in fact one Dumont who filed patents some thirty years later, in the early 1860s, for the use of photographs in a zootrope toy and is therefore the first person on record to understand the potential of photography for such devices.[14]

Other errors arise because of the selectivity of detail, which is, again, conditioned by 'great man' considerations. Here the major thematic omission has to do with economics. For example, Scott Archer did not die penniless because he was feckless and naive. Rather it was because he was pursued through the courts by Fox-Talbot for infringement of patent.[15] The state eventually provided an annuity of £50 per annum to Scott Archer's children.[16] The stripping away of such commercial quotidian details serves to elevate the account into a realm of pure creativity and progress with one savant building on the work of another. The reality is often quite other as the next phase of the received history – the dry plate element – illustrates.

Gelatin, for example, was suggested by a number of investigators in the twenty years before Maddox, and, after the Hyatts produced the first semi-rigid sheets in 1869, numerous workers apart from Eastman thought to exploit its potential. Notable among these was the Reverend Hannibal Goodwin of New Jersey who sought a patent for flexible transparent film in 1887. Under American patent law, other workers can object to a grant of patent if they can demonstrate that the proposal in some way interferes with their patents and investigations.[17] As a result of these interference procedures, Goodwin's patent was delayed for eleven years during which time the chief among those objecting to him, the Eastman Kodak Company, not only claimed interference but also applied for its own patents covering celluloid film and a specific manufacturing process as well. Goodwin won but he could not afford to pursue Kodak through the courts in his turn for infringement so he assigned his rights to the Ansco Company of New York. He died two years later in 1900 with this case still unresolved, his only reward a small amount of cash and a block of Ansco shares. Eventually, in 1914, Ansco won and received millions of dollars from Kodak for its illegal use of a process George Eastman did not 'invent' but nevertheless ruthlessly exploited.[18] The same sort of legal battles occupied the pioneers of the cinema proper.

The Edison Patent Battles
These conflicts turn on Edison's personal claim to have 'invented' motion pictures. I have already indicated that both Muybridge and Marey were involved in talking to him about, at the very minimum, stop-motion techniques. Muybridge was also in contact with Marey. Marey's multiple-image camera was also prefigured, it can be noted, by Janssen who had developed a similar device – like Marey's termed a revolver – in 1874, fourteen years earlier than Marey.[19] Like Muybridge, Janssen was in touch with Marey.

And there is also the question of the exact role of W. K. L. Dickson, 'a young laboratory assistant who was keen on photography', who was actually conducting the day-to-day research and development programme in Edison's West Orange lab that led to the Kinetoscope. Gordon Hendricks, a modern historian whose pursuit of Edison's pretensions and mendacities borders on a crusade,[20] wishes to write Dickson in as the real innovator, substituting him for Edison in an alternative 'great man' explanation.[21] This is because others want to attribute the whole of Dickson's labour to Edison.[22] Hendricks not only seeks to correct this but also to attack the 'Wizard's' overall claim to the 'invention' of cinematography. For example, Hendricks is dismissive of a sketch in Edison's own hand of a film strip with sprocket holes in a caveat dated 2 November 1889, the best evidence for such a claim. (In US law, a caveat is a pre-patent notice of work in progress which acts to bar other experimenters.)

There is little point in attempting to arbitrate between Edison and Dickson and their partisans. It is more fruitful to see Edison's West Orange laboratory, like the enterprise set up by Bayer in Germany, as being among the first research organisations designed to explore commercial exploitations of innovation. As with its state-funded predecessors, such as the Conservatoire des Arts et Métiers established in Paris in 1799, a number of research programmes could be undertaken at once and by a large number of hands.[23] The scale of the Edison lab meant many people were involved in any individual project – more than 200 on the light bulb, for example.[24] Although involving far fewer workers, cinematography was in like case and was certainly not at the forefront of Edison's personal concerns.

There is, however, yet another figure whose contribution can also be used to dispute Edison's innovative ingenuity. William Friese-Greene began his researches in Bath into the representation of motion with a series of devices for the rapid projection of slides involving multiple magic lanterns, or multiple lenses. In January 1888 he was using oiled photographic paper strips, as in the obsolete calotype process, but with sprocket holes, to make 300 images at about ten per second. He patented his camera in June 1889, describing it therein as using a 'roll of any convenient length of sensitized paper or the like'.[25] 'Or the like', of course, was celluloid and although there has been some doubt about whether or not Friese-Green got to the celluloid strip before Edison, Michael Chanan has testimony that he was using it in a projector in 1889. Further, Hendricks has discovered that Friese-Greene, like Muybridge, was in touch with Edison. In March, 1890 he wrote to say he was sending a description of his camera.[26] On the basis of his British legal position, Friese-Greene was able to obtain a declaration that his was the master patent for cinematography and that some of Edison's claims should be set aside.

But, as with Scott Archer and Goodwin and despite the insistence of patent law (and the great man approach to technological history) on primacy, Friese-Greene did not 'win'. As Janet Staiger puts it: 'Technically, patent law suggests that the value issuing from an invention should go to its originator. However, access to legal restitution is not equal. Unless the inventor has sufficient capital to pursue rights, they are unenforceable.'[27] Edison had attempted to license all exploitation of sprocketed 35mm and he was able to maintain his dominance even against set-backs like the Friese-Greene decision. He did this because his licensing system had a real sanction built into it:

Eastman was his ally and would not deal with unlicensed production and exhibition entities. This was effective because, although others were manufacturing dry photographic materials on celluloid, and although Eastman was, as we have seen, also involved in a serious patent battle, his manufacturing techniques were nevertheless capable of producing easily the most suitable (i.e. the thinnest) films for cinematography. Not only this, the Lumières were using 35mm for no better reason than that they had seen the gauge in the Kinetoscope.[28]

So important was all this that the limitations of 35mm were ignored. Those exploiting the Edison Vitascope, which was in essence projected Kinetoscope strips, suggested to Arnat in 1896 that a larger-gauge film be used 'simply to enable us to make a picture of proper width to exhibit on a theatrical stage'.[29] But this could not be done without endangering the patent position. Conversely, the Biograph (and its peep-show version, the Mutograph), which were introduced by the Mutoscope Company – a group including Dickson who had now split from Edison – used unperforated 70mm film. This was exactly better to serve the large vaudeville house – and to avoid, for patent reasons, 35mm and sprocket holes. By 1897, 70mm was the preferred technology at least in the United States in 'first class theatres'.[30] Edison's licensees were left with the rest of the market. However, with the *de facto* support of the Lumières and the superiority of the Eastman process also behind him, Edison and 35mm came to dominate.

The received story has the great men Edison and Eastman instantly responding to each other to allow the latter to play a 'leading role' in the creation of cinematography,[31] with Eastman supposedly being in at the start. Eastman wrote in 1925 that: 'The idea of making pictures to depict objects in motion was entirely new to me but of course I was much interested in the project and did my best to furnish him [Edison] film as near to his specifications.'[32] But these were not Edison's specifications, nor was Eastman initially involved.

Dickson had been experimenting with commercially available sheets from another manufacturer, Carbutt. When the work moved to strips, Dickson began with a ³/₄" (19mm) one.[33] The initial order from the Edison Laboratory in West Orange to the Kodak Company in Rochester for such a strip of film was addressed to 'Eastman and Co.' and called for a 'Kodac [sic] transparent film ³/₄" wide and as long as possible'. It was signed 'W. K. L. Dickson'.[34] Dickson went twice to Rochester to secure the necessary material, the first time dealing with the firm in general; George Eastman, contrary to his own account, was initially unaware of this approach.

Edison had pressing business reasons for establishing that he was using 35mm as early and as unambiguously as he could. Thirty or more years after these events, these reasons were still conditioning his memory. Thus, in the memoir which he also wrote for the thirtieth anniversary of the cinema in 1925, he stated that he used 35mm from the very start of serious experimentation: 'I then experimented with photographs one inch wide by three-quarters of an inch high. These dimensions were adopted by me in 1889 and remain today the standard of the art.'[35] Simply untrue; but it is easy to see why, after the patent wars with Biograph and others, such a narrative would lodge in his mind – and in the minds of others too. Thus Dickson's depersonalised communication to the Kodak company becomes, in some accounts, a letter from Edison[36] while one article in the *SMPTE Journal* goes so far as to suggest that the *initial* Dickson letter actually called for 'a roll of film 35mm in width' to be sent to New Jersey.[37]

After the turn of the century, the pressure to standardise was backed up by Edison's legal aggression which was expressed through the twenty-three infringement suits his lawyers started before 1901. This barrage did not quite ensure that all film firms became Edison licensees because some, notably Biograph, had acquired projector patents of their own upon which they counter-claimed Edison was infringing. Nevertheless, the net result was to confirm 35mm's hegemony.[38] Burton Holmes, a pioneer of the documentary lecture film who coined the term 'travelogue',[39] switched from 60mm to 35mm in 1902. Biograph itself, hiding behind its acquired projector patents, started to use 35mm in 1903/4[40] and the company consolidated its position as a major producer, eventually home to D. W. Griffith for the first phase of his career. But not on 70mm.[41] Biograph's pricing policy, which claimed a premium for its superior image, also helped Edison. Within eight years the matter was settled in 35mm's favour. Biograph (or anybody else for that matter) had to conform to the gauge (if not to Edison's financial imposts) if they were to maximise their business.

Four years later, in 1908, a final attempt to impose a licence-based monopoly was mounted after Edison and Biograph resolved their patent stand-off with a cross-licensing agreement. This enabled them to establish the Motion Picture Patents Company, known as the MPPC, or the 'Trust', which consolidated its position by signing an exclusive deal with Eastman Kodak for celluloid and by creating a subsidiary to organise a nationwide distribution system for films. It was this last which provoked a response in the form of a trade association which rapidly became a rival distribution company.[42]

In this environment of flying writs, equipment impoundments and injunctions, a Friese-Greene becomes useful to others. They could and did use him and everybody else who contributed to the creation of the motion picture system of dry-film manufacturing, stock gauge, perforation techniques and perforation standards, cameras, developing and printing apparatus and projectors as legal sticks with which to beat Edison. (Friese-Greene, though, was not to be allowed to turn into a substitute for Edison and thereby become another potentially repressive licenser, which is why he never made any money). The result was a state of considerable legal flux. Even in the matter of the stock, upon which Edison's claims seemed to be most securely founded, he turned out to be vulnerable, his patent being declared void in 1912.[43] But he was not so much vulnerable to individuals, who were likely, as was Friese-Greene, to lack the resources to pursue him, but to combinations of rival firms, who might, exactly, command such resources.

The patents of the Motion Picture Patents Company rapidly proved a less than perfect basis for a monopoly and, because of anti-trust legislation, the very fact of combination was even more flawed. The Justice Department sued the MPPC under the anti-trust Sherman Act in 1912. The court found for the Government in 1915 but long before that the attempt to maintain monopoly was failing. The impact of other private anti-trust suits played a role here and also, suggests Janet Staiger, some MPPC companies were distancing themselves by marketing the newly developed multiple-reel film outside the Trust's distribution structures.[44] The MPPC was declared illegal in 1917. Cinema had arrived as a fully diffused technology.

The Context for Cinema: Realism and Illusionism

But to take cognisance of such terms of trade is only the beginning of what must be done to correct the overall errors of the received history. Simply putting in every last great (and least) man will not serve,[45] nor will it be sufficient to just add non-Western elements and economics. In the last decades, there has been an on-going attempt to provide an appropriately rich social context for the emergence of the cinema.[46] So we must return to the beginning once more for an account of these elements.

Central to this attempt to make the technological an expression of the social is the idea of cinema being part of a centuries-old Western project to create what A. D. Coleman has called 'lens culture'.[47] This implies a particular set of social practices whereby a viewer relates to a screen. These determine the cultural dimension of the Western way of seeing even though the devices involved might have initially been Eastern innovations.

The first great triumph of this way of seeing is the creation of various modes of representation of space on flat surfaces, including the *construzione legittima* of Alberti mentioned above. (This is not the first such system to be used, however, there being a number even within the Western tradition that can be discerned between ancient times and the 14th century[48] and, of course, the northern Europeans produced a rival 'distant point construction' of perspective first described by Viator in *Artificiali perspectiva* (1505), which is the basis of Dutch seventeenth-century painting.[49])

The Renaissance deployment of perspective impacts on the social sphere in ways that are critical to all subsequent developments of the lens culture of the West. For example, it establishes a preference for certain forms of realistic modes of pictorial representation which are (or tend to be) illusionist. The desire for this illusionist simulacrum of the external world feeds the entire research agenda from Alberti through the magic lantern to the cinema and on into the present; from painting to photography (which released painting from the prison of realism) to the cinema and, again, on into the present. Considered dispassionately, it could be said that this realism of the West is a somewhat dull thing, incarcerating image-making within the bounds of the forms of the external world. Be that as it may, it is crucial for our understanding of modern systems of representation, including the cinema.

The triumph of Renaissance perspective systems, especially the Italian, also involves another profound social effect in that such systems required that the eye be locked into a certain position in order for the illusion to be perceived. This was literally true of Brunelleschi's painting of the Baptistery in Florence, conventionally the earliest image, now lost, to use the newly minted perspective system that Alberti described. The painting was executed on a wood panel:

> At the centre of the picture of the Baptistery there was a small hole which opened into a funnel on the back of the panel. The viewer stood behind the panel and looked through the funnel at a mirror held at arm's length in front of it. The mirror reflected the painting, and the results ... were astonishing. A powerful abstraction had been created whereby the painter compelled the viewer to see nothing but what he wished him to see.[50]

It is this locking, the rationalisation of sight as it has been termed,[51] that conditions Western publics to perceive space through the use of particular codes of representation on flat surfaces. This was a crucial lesson for these publics and a vital precondition for the popularity of the magic lantern, photography and cinematography.

The realism of the Renaissance underwent many stylistic changes in the course of the next several centuries but one can note that, at the moment of photograph, painting was itself in the grip of an extremely realistic movement. Indeed, the term 'realism' in art history conventionally means exactly a group of nineteenth-century painters, led by Courbet, who supposedly went beyond mere naturalism ('which is no more than the simple-minded pleasure in being able to make an accurate transcript of nature') to the 'search for the squalid and the depressing as a means of life enhancement'.[52] Lynda Nochlin persuasively makes the case that this conventional view is inadequate and that, in fact, the aim of this movement, between 1840 and 1870–80, was rather 'to give a truthful, objective and impartial representation of the real world, based on meticulous observation of contemporary life'.[53] In other words, exactly what photography was supposed to do. As the century progressed, photography moved from being an aid to such realistic painting[54] to being its nemesis. On hearing about the daguerreotype one painter, perhaps just a little prematurely, announced: 'From today painting is dead.'[55] Painting with the sort of purpose Nochlin adduces to realism was, if not to die at photography's hand, then certainly to be battered by it.

The embedding of these aesthetic strategies and preferences into Western taste over the past half-millennium can be said to indicate a species of addiction – an addiction to realism. This addiction which produced Renaissance perspective painting also deeply affected the development of the Western theatre.

The theatre, even before it moved indoors, used props and elements of scenery. In the 17th century, it became a major site of perspective illusionism, first in the interests of neoclassicism but then, throughout the 18th and 19th centuries, in the interests of an ever more naturalistic realism. The coming of gas lighting to the Theatre Royal, Drury Lane, and the Lyceum Opera in 1817 further fed the illusionist addiction[56]:

> Second only to lighting among theatrical innovations was the growing demand for more lavishly realistic scenic spectacle. ... To meet this demand,

theatre architects and their engineering consultants translated the floor area of their stages into a kind of jigsaw puzzle ... German and American engineers provided double stages; an earlier British innovation was the provision of aquatic facilities for the representation of naval battles, river crossings, and other heroic incidents. ... Without the aid of such technological advances Wagner could hardly have required the Rhine to overflow its banks, or the Palace of the Valhalla to come crashing to the ground when *Der Ring des Nibelungen* was given its first complete performance in the purpose-built Festspielhaus at Bayreuth in 1876. By the end of the century, revolving stages carrying three different stage-settings could replace one another within a few seconds at the touch of a button.[57]

The taste for scenery was so extreme that it alone could sustain a show. First to exploit this was the Panorama, devised in 1787, where audiences were surrounded by a painting 16ft high or so which slowly circled the seats. The display was accompanied by commentary and effects. Then, from Louis Daguerre and his partner Charles Button, came a more sophisticated variant of this, the Diorama. Here the audience was transported before a scene in which there was movement and elaborate light changes as well as music, sound effects and commentary and, in the foreground, real objects like models of chalets and fir trees to give depth to the image of, say, Mont Blanc behind.[58]

Chanan, following Walter Benjamin, suggests that these entertainments were essentially both 'philistine' and 'middle class' (that is, presumably, both lowbrow and respectable), representing a recovery of the countryside these recently urbanised audiences had lost as well as a celebration of the cityscapes they had gained. The Dioramas, wrote Benjamin, were 'the *locus* of a perfect imitation of nature'.[59] Such spectacles were a most salient site of the modern as well as being exempla of what Jean-Louis Comolli describes as a 'sort of frenzy of the visible' which was then gripping the industrialising world.[60] Obviously, this returns us to the magic lantern, albeit writ large; and, indeed, projected photographs were used in these spectacles before they were put into the 'wheel of life' toys.

Magic lantern shows are recorded from the 17th century on. By the late 18th century the physical circumstances in which the projected image was to be viewed in this culture had been determined. Instead of the casual displays of earlier times, Étienne Gaspar Robertson, who shocked audiences in revolutionary Paris with *Fantasmagorie*, a magic lantern show of ghosts and ghouls, sat his audience in rows in the dark before the screen.[61] (The coming of gaslight to the theatres also allowed for the darkening of the auditorium for the first time at live entertainments.) As the 19th century progressed the lantern's beam became more and more intense, even before the introduction of the electric lamp. Limelight was used from 1822. By 1885 calcium light projectors were available. The magic lantern slide became more complex by means of simple animations while by 1857 at the latest came what John Fell called 'the integration of auditorium and photography'. In that year two battle Panoramas of Sebastopol and Solferino used photographic slides.[62]

(There was another way in which the early-nineteenth-century theatre prepared people for such more or less purely visual shows. In a number of European countries, theatres were licensed and controlled but legal definitions required actors to speak. To avoid this control, a fashion grew up for (unlicensed) melodramatic dumb-shows, mimed to music with placards to explain the action.[63])

The operation of this addiction to realism thus created in the social sphere a number of elements which were to be crucial to the cinema. Before the turn of the 19th century, the public was prepared to be entertained by being seated in rows in a darkened space to look at magic lantern slides. After the coming of the gaslamp, auditoria for live spectacles were also darkened. A taste for dumb show was in vogue. These live spectacles involved highly realistic effects and some entertainments consisted entirely of displays of realistic scenery, animated and augmented in various ways short of live acting. What characterises these last is an extreme verisimilitude, an expression of the sort of public pictorial taste that had dominated in the West for the previous several centuries.

The Context for Cinema: Narrative

But there are other elements of the same kind, which demand attention if the context for cinema is to be explicated. There is a second sort of addiction relating to spectacle in the West. It is less obvious and more contentious than is the dominance of a realistic mode of representation but it is nevertheless crucial: narrative. On the one hand, it is clear that, although there are exceptions, the broad theatrical tendency is to narrative, and this is true even of the most purely spectacular of forms such as the Panorama and Diorama. Of these, John Fell has written: 'All such performances, of course, show unity of time and space, but soon we note a developing sense of sequence and selection of detail, as well as the introduction of movement within a scene.'[64]

There is a sense in which this should hardly be surprising. There are those who would argue the propensity to narrative is closely and inextricably bound up with the fundamental human ability to communicate. To speak is to narrate; and to listen and to look is to seek constantly to establish logical and chronological connections – to attempt narrative order out of chaos.[65] This is, of course, to understand narrative in a very broad sense; but not, I believe, to take it beyond where current narratology would have it.

For instance, the mark of narrative as a distinct text type is, as Seymour Chatman says, that it '*temporally* controls its reception by audience' and, moreover, does so logically. The slowly moving audience of the Diorama was obviously being controlled temporally, if not – as when simple scenery was on display – logically. However, when the Diorama displayed, say, the course of a battle, then logic also came into play and the result is what Chatman calls a 'chrono-logic'.[66] Chatman distinguishes a number of text types – 'mere description', 'argument' and 'explanation' as well as 'narrative'. The temporal control element in the Diorama means that its 'text' is beyond 'mere description' while the visual display means it is also beyond 'argument' and, largely, beyond 'explanation'. So, as texts, many Dioramas

25

were beyond argument, description and explanation and are therefore most safely and appropriately characterised as a species of narrative.

Narrative was everywhere in the world of nineteenth-century screen practice – from the animated peep-show which grew out of the 'wheels of life' to the sequenced slides of the magic lantern show. Although often the effects stood alone – Robespierre rising from the tomb was a big hit with the Fantasmogorie audience – the world of the magic lantern was no more adverse to narrative than predecessor image-making regimes – church imagery as when it dealt with the life of Christ, for example. One of the very earliest of recorded magic lantern shows involved a journey – a basic narrative form – to China.[67] By the 19th century, the slide show involved not only sequences but a panoply of techniques for melding the images together. All of the elements that were to characterise the cinema's methods of transition between shots – cuts, dissolves – were all prefigured in the lantern show. (Descriptive title cards were picked up from the dumb-shows.)

This propensity to arrange images in a logical order and then to display them at a fixed pace before an audience is, at the very least, a mark or trace of the addiction to narrative. As such it renders moot the argument of the last decade or so as to how much such narratives were carried forward into the early cinema and whether or not the cinema took at some point 'a narrative turn', having initially been a non-narrative form. These long-standing tendencies within the social sphere in general and the practice of spectacle (including screen spectacle) in particular suggest that this is not the case. It is rather, if you will, that the cinema failed to struggle against millennia of storytelling and centuries of régimes of sequenced pictorial representation.[68]

Moreover, at the very beginning, single-shot films were arranged for exhibition interspersed with slides to fill the screen during reloading – not perhaps involving a logic of causality but certainly with a sense of the need to maintain at least one level of temporal continuity – 'audience time' as it were.[69] Stephen Bottomore further suggests that this habit of sequencing then led to the creation of film editing whereby a single-shot film, analogous to a slide, was joined with others to create a sequence of shots analogous to a slide sequence – although spacing was inserted to avoid 'jerks' or 'shocks to the eye'. He points out that at the very beginning '"cinematographic slides" was a common term for films'. The British pioneer Cecil Hepworth suggested 'stringing the images together into little sets or episodes'.[70] By 1897 an event such as the Spanish-American War was featured in a display using twenty films and slides. Before 1900 a twenty-shot film had been made by Méliès – *Cendrillon*. In Australia in 1900, thirteen short films and two hundred slides were constituted into a show which lasted for more than two hours.[71]

Narrative is not the inevitable destiny of the cinema – it is just that it is the inevitable destiny of any cinema created in a Western culture addicted to narrative – i.e. the only cinema there is.

The Context for Cinema: The Mass Audience
One last crucial context for the 'invention' of the cinema can now be considered – the 'invention' (as it might be termed) of the modern

audience. Beyond the technology, beyond addictions to realism and narrative as they might infect individuals within the culture, is this matter of the mass audience.

As we have seen, the audience by the middle years of the 19th century had long since learned to sit in rows in darkened auditoria. Now it grew ever larger as the rural population drifted to the city. Population in general had already doubled and tripled in the first half of the century in the industrialising world. In the United States, thanks to immigration, it had increased six-fold.[72] The result overall was that between 1800 and 1850, European city-dwellers increased from 10 per cent of the population to 16.7 per cent.[73] By 1851 Britain, the most urbanised society, became the first country where the total population of cities and towns was greater than the rural population – 51 per cent. In the next three decades, the great cities themselves doubled and trebled in size.[74] By 1900 only 36 per cent of Germans and 43 per cent of the French still lived on the land.[75] By now Europe as a whole was 29 per cent urban; in England and Wales the figure was 61.9 per cent. The mass audience had arrived. As Eric Hobsbawm states: 'At some point in the later 19th century the mass migration into the rapidly growing big cities produced ... a lucrative market for popular spectacle.'[76] Meeting the demand created by this mass (for whom the prospect of spectacle and stimulation was as much bound up with the urban and the modern as was the opportunity for new sorts of work) required the industrialisation of many forms of entertainment and communication.

Take newspapers. In Great Britain, for example, these describe a trajectory from the artisanal to the industrial as journalistic and publishing functions become specialised. Instead of a Defoe or a Cobbett working virtually single-handed, writing every word for a small paper to be printed, 1,200 copies an hour, on a flat-bed press that had in essence remained unchanged for several centuries, there now emerges a reporter, an editor, a publisher, printers and so on. There were specialisations of technique – e.g. the wide use of shorthand in reporting – and technology – e.g. the application of steam power in the rotary press and the use of the telegraph. By the middle years of the 19th century, newspapers had transformed themselves from small-scale enterprises with uncontrollable and unpredictable political and social effects into large, capital-intensive operations, belonging to and controlled by a class of citizen concerned both to make profits and to exercise social control in favour of the established order. In this way, newspapers were rendered so safe for capital exploitation that all the failing systems of state control, the licences and the special 'taxes on knowledge', which anyway had not prevented the growth of an unlicensed press, could then be safely removed, as indeed they were by 1862.[77]

The newspaper found its readership in the growing cities but it also, because of the railways, reached out into smaller centres of population in order to maximise its business. The theatre needed the final flood of people to arrive in the city itself to achieve the same level of industrialisation. Parallel developments in the theatre therefore tended to run some decades behind those in the press. Nevertheless, the same pattern can be seen in the theatre whereby failing state controls also eventually give way to apparently liberalised, centralised and capital-intensive operations.

In Britain, the slow disappearance of the street entertainer, the increasing marginalisation of the fair and the rise of the music hall all worked to turn popular theatrical entertainment into a collective urban experience.[78] The taste for collective activity provided by places of entertainment was reinforced, Chanan claims, by other developments, notably the mass Chartist movement which brought people together for political purposes. The needs of an industrialised society required that this mass be educated, which in its turn increased the need for mass information and entertainment systems. As Raymond Williams pointed out, the pressures for such education antedated its formal provision by decades, but 'we need to remember that the new institutions were not produced by the working people themselves. They were, rather, produced for them by others, often (as most notably with the cheap newspaper and commercial advertisement on a large scale) for conscious political or commercial advantage.'[79]

In the theatre, as with newspapers, this move was marked by the emergence of new specialists. By the late 18th century, individually owned theatres were organised into 'tours'. These were sometimes virtually the property of one actor-manager. The Yorkshire circuit, for example, grew from the regular rotation through the county of one group of players led by Tate Wilkinson. Forced often to play in ordinary rooms in inns, he began to build theatres in the 1770s. City corporations were also moved to erect theatres. By the 1780s a full circuit had been created.

Wilkinson, although a former actor, was an example of the new breed of manager who did not perform as against the older actor-manager who appeared in shows which he produced (i.e. directed) and with companies which he organized. The actor-manager then dominated the theatre and has never quite died out even into the present day (e.g. Kenneth Branagh). However, Wilkinson's basic organisation was still quite primitive with only his company playing in these theatres and then only for fixed seasons, normally arranged to coincide with other events such as the races or the assizes.[80]

More complex forms of organisation were also emerging at this time. The Theatre Royal, Bristol (now Britain's oldest working theatre), 'was partner in the most prosperous and prestigious provincial circuit in the country, that created by John Palmer and William Keasberry of Bath from 1779 onwards'.[80] Keasberry was an actor-manager in the old style, but his partner, Palmer, was more like Wilkinson albeit in a more extreme form – a backroom administrator who neither acted nor produced.

Nevertheless, even Palmer was still deeply involved in the business of managing actors. Logically, a further step could be taken and was when a new form of manager arose out of these 'tours'; this was a person who did not act and manage (as did Keasberry) nor only manage (as did Palmer) but who just owned the bricks and mortar. One show in many theatres, instead of each theatre producing its own shows, was starting to make economic sense. One group of managers produced the product, the other group marketed it. In America, from the 1840s on, the môde of production was the stock company. Unlike old-style wandering players, the stock company eschewed repertory and instead played the same show for limited runs in an established circuit of venues.

As the 19th century advanced, the sense of this more highly developed organisational structure became inescapable:

> By taking advantage of railways and fast ocean liners, managers were discovering that instead of waiting for audiences to turn up at their theatres, productions could be transported to the audiences in equally well-equipped theatres at home and abroad with an actor or actress (sometimes both) at the head of the company whose personal reputation was sure to attract crowds where ever they appeared. This attracted businessmen with little or no experience of the theatre, but with a flair for anticipating public taste, to enter into theatre management by acquiring chains of theatre buildings.[82]

The consequences of this division of labour were immense. The 'star' system, already in embryo because of the nature of previous production structures, becomes an essential marketing element of the new system. Long runs become possible. The artistic control of the production gets spun off into the hands of a producer (or, as this person was to become known, the director).[83] Booking agents, talent agents, publicists and so on all followed. Augustin Daly was the first entrepreneur in the USA to assemble a chain of theatres and he was in Britain followed by Sir Edward Moss and Sir Oswald Stoll.

As these British knighthoods eloquently suggest, such men of property were a long way from the 'rogues, vagabonds and players' of previous centuries. And, as happened with newspapers after they were safely in the hands of men of property, the legislation on theatres moved from draconian, if inefficient, control to a régime that aided and abetted the entrepreneurs. First, the Theatre Act of 1843 removed the royal monopoly at the two London Patent Theatres (the Theatres Royal, Drury Lane and Haymarket). Moreover, as with any other industry in Victorian Britain, the theatre was subjected to parliamentary inquiry. The 'Suitability Act' of 1878, arising from such investigation, was designed as a public safety measure by instituting the legal requirement that all theatres have iron safety curtains.[84] But the Act had other effects, especially on the music-halls.

These had spent the first half of the century emerging from a tradition of 'free and easy' sing-songs at the pub. One London publican, Charles Morton, had built a specialised hall adjacent to his tavern in 1852 to bring a measure of formality to these occasions. Over the next two decades such halls or Theatres of Variety proliferated, but after the Licensing Act of 1878 ... the number of independent theatres fell as management companies took them over. As a result, artistes were increasingly booked not for appearances in individual theatres but for tours which included several. Agents consequently grew more powerful.'[85] Two hundred halls were closed and many more, whose owners could not afford to meet the safety requirements, slipped into chain ownership. By the mid-1890s, both legitimate theatres and these music-halls (in America, vaudevilles), which by now had become identical to them physically, had been industrialised. The stage had been transformed from what was in the 1860s just a 'show' (a term new at that time) into what was by the 1890s 'show business' (a phrase new at that time).

The same sort of sequence of developments can be seen elsewhere. Eighteenth-century forms such as 'the popular suburban theatre in Vienna, the dialect theatre in the Italian cities, the popular (as distinct from court) opera, the commedia dell'arte and travelling mime show'[86] could welcome the ever-increasing urban throngs as easily as did the English-speaking music-hall or vaudeville. By the 1850s, all these popular theatrical forms had become fixtures in the European city. Two decades of urbanisation on and, Hobsbawm claims, among the German-speaking peoples 'operas and theatres became temples in which men and women worshipped'.[87] These could be 'the focus of town planning as in Paris (1860) and Vienna (1869), visible as cathedrals as in Dresden (1869), invariably gigantic and monumentally elaborate as in Barcelona (from 1862) or Palermo (from 1875)'.[88] The demand for theatre in many of these places was met as part of general municipal development rather than as the result of entrepreneurial endeavour. German theatres, originally mainly trophy structures for the dukes and princelings who had ruled the German mini-states, tripled in numbers between 1870 and 1896.[89] Many of these were municipal.[90]

These new structures, both physical and organisational, conformed the theatre to capitalist practice and produced industrial institutions identical to those of any other sector – cartels, for example. At a secret meeting in 1895, ostensibly to bring some order to the American booking situation, a group of agents, managers (including Charles Frohman, who had pioneered road shows, that is, the concept of duplicate touring productions) and theatre-chain owners established the Theatrical Syndicate. Rapidly, the Syndicate (also known as the Theatrical Trust) established a stranglehold on the entire American legitimate theatre.

Vaudeville was a little behind, still seeking in the 1880s to distance itself from the less salubrious aspects of its origins (which were to become burlesque). Benjamin Keith and Edward Albee were responsible for a cleaned-up variety show which all members of a family could attend. They also built the first chain of theatres to house their innovation. By the mid-1890s there were five major chains covering the larger cities.[91] Robert Allen estimates at least a million people a week went to the vaudeville by 1896.[92] The owners formed themselves into an Association of Vaudeville Managers, parallel to the Theatrical Trust, in 1900 and achieved a similar effect in this sector.

If the owners, producers and agents organised themselves, so did theatrical workers. Benevolent funds for indigent actors were established in Britain and America by the early 1880s. These were followed by trade unions proper. In the United States, actors in 1895 formed themselves into the Actors' Society of America in response to the Theatrical Syndicate. This gave way to Actor's Equity in 1912/13. In Britain, the ancient Worshipful Company of Musicians, which had been moribund from the mid-18th century, became in 1891 the London Orchestral Association after a number of false starts over the previous two decades. It has survived, in the form of the Musicians' Union, into the present. The first Actor's Association in Britain was also formed in this year but was short-lived. Nevertheless other attempts followed, eventually producing the Actors' Society, the direct precursor of British Actors' Equity. The Theatrical and Music Hall Operatives' Trade Union (which organised carpenters and other backstage workers) was in place before 1900. The Variety Artists Association was founded in 1902.[93] And there were strikes. In 1901 the White Rats, who were the American equivalent of the British Variety Artists Association, struck the Association of Vaudeville Managers.[94] As an industrialised business, the theatre had come of age.

Over the century before the coming of the cinema, theatrical delivery systems (as it were) were extended to maximise markets. Product was differentiated, often with quite distinct class connotations, although the theatre remained more a place of common resort than did many other public sites of the time, albeit with the commoner sort 'up in the gods' and the well-to-do below. Niches were covered so that every last possible audience could be drawn into the theatre. At the very end of the day (or of the line), 'tent shows' of broad Victorian farce and variety were still touring the backroads of rural America well into the middle decades of the 20th century. Variety survived World War II in London. But the central point is that by 1895, the broad mass of the audience, addicted to naturalistic illusion and narrative, was sitting in the darkened seats of the auditorium watching highly professional entertainments created by a logistically complex, capital-intensive, if somewhat risky, industry. Both the producers and the consumers of this product were waiting for the cinema.

Towards a Structural Account of the Making of Cinema

It is then in this sense that we can say it was the audience, as much as anything else, which 'invented' the cinema in the mid-1890s. This is the answer to Bazin's fundamental question: 'How was it that the invention took so long to emerge, since all the prerequisites had been assembled ... ?'[95] Bazin provocatively goes on to draw attention to the possible extent of this delay: 'The photographic cinema could just as well have grafted itself on to a phenakistoscope foreseen as long ago as the 16th century. The delay in the invention of the latter is as disturbing a phenomenon as the existence of the precursors of the former.'

Most commentators do not acknowledge a delay. The technology is deemed to appear as soon as all the technical elements involved were available. Thus, one such commentator writes: 'The moving photograph did not become technically feasible until about 1890.' [96] More specifically:

Technological opportunity is the consequence of the historical stage of development which has been reached by the material forces of production. In the case of cinematography, the main factors were the improvement of photographic emulsions; the development of precision engineering and

31

instruments, and their application to the problem of the intermittent drive mechanism; the development of the chemicals industry involved in the quite unconnected invention of celluloid – the first of the plastics – and the improvement of its production techniques to the point where it became available as a thin film, durable, flexible and transparent enough to provide the base for the film strip.[97]

Yet, how many of these requirements were really not available until the 1890s? How many were to hand ten, twenty or even thirty years previously?

The notion that the cinema required advances in engineering is not persuasive. As Bazin observed, the mechanisms involved were 'far less complicated than an 18th-century clock'.[98] The engineering available in the mid-century might not have been quite refined enough to create a full-scale difference engine; but it was more than adequate for the cinema, its cameras/projectors and even its film-stock manufacturing machinery.[99] Somewhat more convincing is an argument that points to the lack of celluloid sheets and films sensitive enough to record an image at a fraction of a second prior to the last decades of the century. Nevertheless, celluloid was being developed in the late 1840s and anyway, as Friese-Greene demonstrated, there were other possible, if less effective, flexible bases available. Furthermore, following Godard's innovation of 1840, silver bromide's potential as a chemical to increase sensitivity and enable fast exposures was also being explored by the 1860s. This line of experiments needed no conceptual breakthrough or discovery. Thus, even if elements were not actually available before the period 1888 (say) to 1895, nevertheless not enough is 'discovered' then to make the case for the cinema coming into being at the first available 'technological opportunity'. Indeed, the contrary can be claimed: nothing was 'discovered' and Bazin's sense of disturbance is quite justified.

On the other hand, Chanan is entirely correct when he supports his assumption about technological lacks with the observation that 'cinematography could not have been invented earlier ... because it would not have attracted anyone's attention as an opportunity for investment'.[100] In saying this, he is denying what he sees as Bazin's 'inversion of the historical order of causuality' whereby the cinema creates a demand for itself before it is 'invented' rather than the demand being created 'in the same way as any other demand' after the device is to hand.[101] But if this lack of investment opportunity is seen as simply another way of noting the absence of audience (i.e. the still-maturing state of the theatre as a fully-fledged industry), then Bazin and Chanan can be reconciled. This is where, I want to suggest, the model outlined in the introduction can perhaps be of value.

Let us revisit the history of the development of the cinema, placing it within the model, specifically within the social sphere. Here lie the addictions to realism and story, the tradition of collective action and entertainment and the slow democratisation of leisure:

These factors constitute the social sphere in which the creation of the cinema can occur. This process can be thought to start with what I would call

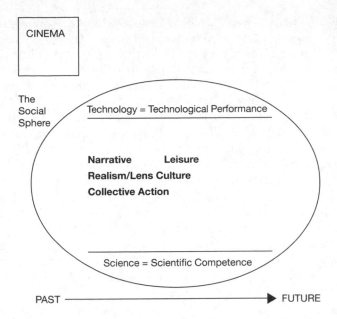

the scientific level of 'competence' – that body of knowledge and collection of devices which together enable a technological 'performance', in this case the 'invention' of cinema, to take place. Essentially, these include the understanding that the eye could be fooled into seeing an illusion of movement, plus the screen practice of the magic lantern plus photography plus celluloid.

The idea of the projected image dates to the 17th century at the latest with what Musser calls Kircher's 'demystification' of the magic lantern. As

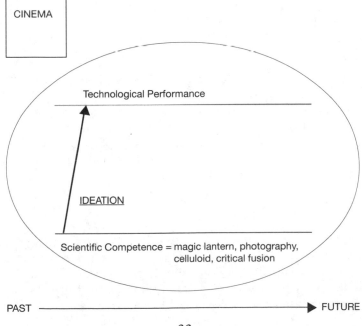

he points out, Kircher's work 'established a relationship between producer, image and audience that has remained fundamentally unaltered ever since'.[103] Gelatine had been suggested as a photographic binding agent by Guadin in 1853.[104] It is used with silver bromide by W. H. Harrison before 1868.[105] The notion of projecting photographs is credited to Charles Langlois (who produced the battle Panoramas mentioned above) by 1857 at the latest. Dumont patented the idea of putting sequences of photographs into a zootrope in the early 1860s. The patent for a shutter in a projector dates to 1869 in the name of A. B. Brown.[105] But did anybody actually have the idea of putting all these elements together before the Lumières?

Louis Ducos du Hauron, whom we will meet again in the next chapter as a pioneer of colour film, patented an 'Apparatus Having for Its Purpose the Photographic Reproduction of Any Kind of a Scene, with All the Changes to Which It Is Subjected during a Specified Time'. He also patented the idea of the photographic strip and that of a projector using a condenser and artificial light. His original patent was sworn out in the French Office on 1 March 1864 but never published, much less built.[106] In this model, this stage is represented by the ideation transformation.

The idea of the cinema, and/or of the elements that would make up the cinema, transform the scientific knowhow, the 'competencies', into a series

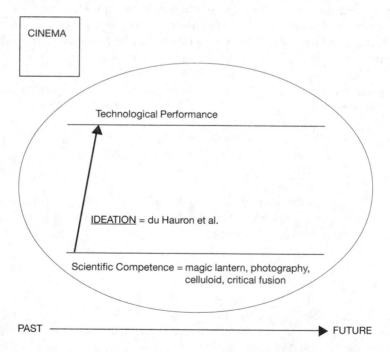

of 'performances' in which devices are built and even sometimes diffused into society. These are prototypes. In the case of the cinema, they include all the Wheels of Life devices up to and including (as it were) the Kinetoscope.

What distinguishes these devices from the 'invention' is the operation of a further transformation.

34

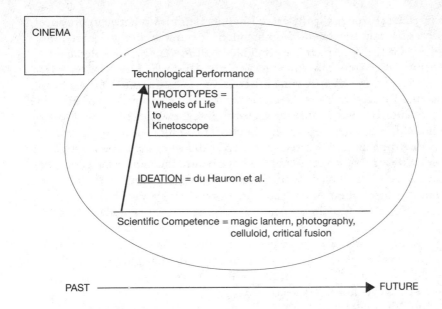

CINEMA

Technological Performance

PROTOTYPES =
Wheels of Life
to
Kinetoscope

IDEATION = du Hauron et al.

Scientific Competence = magic lantern, photography,
celluloid, critical fusion

PAST ⟶ FUTURE

In order to explain the gap between du Hauron and the Lumières, it is necessary to highlight the development of the theatre as the prime factor which changes the situation of the existing technologies and makes the creation of the system we call the cinema viable. It was the industrialisation of the theatre which operated as the supervening social necessity transforming prototypes into invention.

The importance of the theatre to the development of the cinema has been acknowledged by film scholars such as Robert Allen. What I am suggesting here is that particular developments in the 1890s, exemplified by the formations of cartels and unions exactly in the years of the birth of cinema (1895/6), reflect the existence of a large mass audience being served by a highly organised *and recently created* industry. The emergence of this theatrical industry operates as a supervening social necessity to transform the prototype technology and produce the 'invention' – the cinema. It is not just, as Allen writes, that 1895 'was perhaps the most auspicious moment in the history of vaudeville for the introduction of something new'[107]; or that the vaudeville provided 'the infant film industry with a stable marketing outlet during its early years'.[108] It is rather that the existence of this theatrical industry, aided and abetted by dominant late-nineteenth-century notions of modernity, in some measure 'causes' all of the pre-existing technologies to come together as the cinema. It is the new thing in the 1890s: millions of tickets a week.

What du Hauron and all the other pioneers lacked in 1864 (and before) was this supervening necessity, rather than anything technological. (And, as I have pointed out above, one can include in this the critical sensitive flexible celluloid film which was not yet to hand at that date. My point is that Eastman, or better Goodwin, had no competencies that du Hauron lacked.)

So, just as the telegraph runs beside the railways which are its midwife, or the radio appears on the dreadnought battleships which are its midwife, so the cinema appears in the theatre. Although fairgrounds were also a site, they did not prevail as the movies' home. In Britain, after an initial demonstration in the scientifically impeccable confines of the Regent Street Polytechnique, the Cinématographe moved to the Empire Music Hall on 9 March 1896. Sixteen days later, a British version of the Vitascope was part of the bill at the Alhambra Music Hall.[109] In America, 'the Vitascope was presented in various types of entertainment venues, thus extending the eclectic nature of sites already used for motion picture exhibitions'; however, 'vaudeville introduced amusement-goers to projected motion pictures in many major cities.'[110] 'In 1895 Koster & Bial's Music Hall, one of the large vaudeville houses on New York City's Thirty-Fourth Street, first began projecting moving pictures thereby ensuring the commercial success of the new medium. Until about

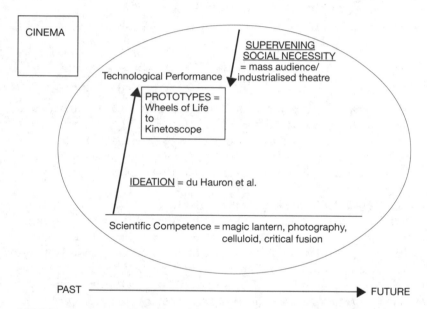

1905 most viewers either saw moving pictures at vaudeville houses such as this or at travelling shows that exhibited at fairgrounds or churches.'[111]

Fairgrounds or amusement parks and theatres were both significant sites but in the long term it was the constant presence of the vaudeville theatres and the music-halls (as opposed to the temporary nature of these other sites) which was critical to ensuring that the cinema became an urban fixture and not a fairground fad.[112] It was the theatre which was selling the tickets week after week. It was the theatre which could import stars: Vesta Tilley, the English male impersonator, was the hit of the 1894 New York season; Yvette Guilbert, the French singer, was paid $3,000 for one week's appearance at Oscar Hammerstein's new Olympia Theatre in 1895.[113] It was the theatre, with its modern electric lights, its plush, its ushers and grand foyers, rather than the ancient semi-rural setting of the fairground, which was to be most appropriate site for the cinema as 'the last [and most modern] machine' of the 19th century.[114] It is no accident that in the founding moments the 'Edison stock-in-trade remained the stage performance extract'.[115] These also figured in the earliest Mutoscope films.[116] Vaudeville was 'the very heart of mainstream mass entertainment ... a complex matrix of commercialised, popular entertainment'.[117]

As significant as the formation of the American theatrical cartel in 1895 was the use of film as a strike-breaking tool in 1901 when the White Rats withdrew their labour from theatres run by members of the Association of Vaudeville Managers. Musser meticulously assesses the evidence for this tactic and concludes that: 'Managers were clearly ready to use films to fight the strike and fill out their bills.'[118] I am not here suggesting that the *raison d'être* for the invention of the cinema was to replace theatre workers. I wish rather to offer these events as symbolic evidence that the theatre and its audience constituted the supervening social necessity for the cinema.

The last transformation, the 'law' of the operation of the suppression of radical potential, obviously does not halt the diffusion of the cinema although it does work to close off a number of potential disruptions.

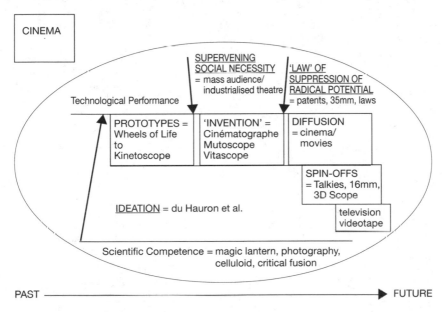

The operation of the patent system (the fights over Edison's claims) works, for example, to conform film production to the previous modes of theatrical organisation with the film exchanges operating not unlike variety booking agents. The establishment of 35mm as the standard limits and professionalises production (about which more will be said in Chapter Three). The application of laws to exhibition sites forces them, expensively, to conform to theatrical norms. The British Cinematographic Act of 1909, for example, echoes the Suitability Act.

As a result, at the end of the process of diffusion, the theatre survived cinema – that is to say, the radical potential of the cinema to destroy the theatre was contained. Not, of course, for ever. I do not claim that the operation of the 'law' of suppression of radical potential brakes developments so hard that no change occurs. Change does occur; but it is slowed so that its impact can be blunted, as was the case here. The result of this transformation was that despite the rapid diffusion of cinema, including theatres being remodelled as cinemas (which in America began early as 1907),[119] the destruction of the popular stage was to take half a century or more to accomplish.

To understand the development of cinema, by all means look to Edison, Lumière and the rest; note economics and social practice; appreciate the importance of cinema to the general concept of modernity. But to answer Bazin's question, that is, to discover why the cinema appears in 1895 and not before, it is necessary to look specifically to the arrival of the urban mass theatrical audience above all; to Frohman and Stoll, the Actors Society and the White Rats; in short, to examine the broader implications of the move from 'show' to 'show business'.

Chapter 2: The Case of Colour Film

White Skin and Colour Film:
The Ideology of the Apparatus

Supervening necessities and the 'law' of constraints - Braudel's accelerators and brakes - speak to one central idea: technology cannot be explained in a social vacuum. It is not an external force to the society, alien and untouched by life around it; rather, it is part and parcel of the society. The history of the development of colour film, the subject of this chapter, shows how deeply social factors can penetrate such development. Essentially, the research agenda for colour film (and more latterly colour television) was dominated by the need to reproduce Caucasian skin tones. This need conditions the ways in which the technologists thought about the competencies made available to them by science, and how they transformed those competencies into actual film stocks. This case offers further evidence of the inadequacy of a technologically determinist approach which would note the work of the scientists involved in the 'invention' of colour film but which would, as it were, fail to note their skin colour.

On Ideological Innocence

The aesthetic has lost its innocence. In current critical discourse it is seen, often as not, as nothing but a willing tool of 'the ideology of the dominant class':

> The aesthetic is for a number of reasons a peculiarly effective ideological medium: it is graphic, immediate and economical, working at instinctual and emotional depths yet playing too on the very surfaces of perception, entwining itself with the stuff of spontaneous experience and the roots of language and gesture. Precisely on this account, it is able to naturalize itself, to proffer itself as ideologically innocent.[1]

In Barthes phrase, it becomes 'ineffable'.[2]

No means of representation is as 'innocent', as 'scientific', as the photograph. Yet, 'every time we look at a photograph, we are aware, however slightly of the photographer selecting that sight from an infinity of other sights.'[3] Moreover, there are factors that go beyond the predilections of the person handling the photographic apparatus to the ideologically charged nature of the apparatus itself. Photographs, cinema and television do not merely express in texts the ideology of the culture that produces them, with the possibility that other ideologies could equally easily be signified in different texts; rather, the technologies are embedded in the social sphere and are themselves an ideological expression of the culture.

It is one such expression – colour film, which more readily photographs Caucasians than other human types – that is my concern here. The point is that colour films are cultural creations. Colours are formed by chemicals known as dye-couplers. The choice of dye-couplers by the chemists designing a film stock will determine the sensitivity of the final product to different lighting conditions and different colours. My contention is that a paramount consideration in this decision-making process will be the ability of the final stock to render 'white' skin in a culturally, and therefore commercially, acceptable manner. This case study is illustrative of the ways in which such ideologically complicit cultural production takes place; how, in effect, cultural conditioning affects the transformation of basic science into technology. In order to demonstrate this I will offer a brief history of the development of colour film including some notes on how the cultural significance of colour has figured in discourses about the cinema. In conclusion, evidence as to the mind-set of chemists involved in the design process, in fact the development of Kodachrome II in the late 1940s and early 50s, will be discussed. But first, let me stress how hidden is the very idea that the cinematographic apparatus carries within it any overt ideology.

At the end of the 1981 documentary *El Pueblo Vencera*,[4] in a mirror-image of the opening scene of the film, a young Salvadoran gun-toting guerrilla in full fatigues encounters an elderly peasant woman, covered basket on head, in a clearing. The woman places her burden on the ground, pulls back the cover and reveals an Arriflex BL 16mm professional film camera which the guerrilla triumphantly exchanges for his gun. The image says that, if once the pen was deemed mightier than the sword, then today the camera can no doubt be thought mightier than the machine-gun. But for this proposition to hold up, a preconditional further point must be admitted, namely that the camera, a product of high West German technology costing some $15,000 at the time the film was made, is a device that can serve, despite its provenance, any communications purpose. Implicit is the idea that, in the context of the politics of El Salvador in the early 80s, or in any other situation, the camera is, in some sense, culturally neutral – just as the gun is neutral.

That the cinema is a child of science and exhibits the supposed objectivity and accuracy of its parent is well known. Cinematography, like photography (and like the camera obscura), was initially introduced to the public as a tool of science and those who worked the new apparatus in each case were '*non tanquam pictor, sed tanquam mathematicus*' (not so much a painter as a mathematician).[5] It is worth noting that these supposed objective qualities are seductive enough to convince many (for whom Diego de la Texera, the director of *El Pueblo Vencera*, can stand), who in different circumstances would be more on the *qui vive* as to the ideological forces with which they are dealing. It is as if de la Texera and other radical film and video-makers have not understood the ideologically imposed limitations of the apparatus. This is, in effect, a type of technological determinism but in the name of a radical political project.

The apparatus of film and television is indeed ideologically limited. It is a product of 'the lens culture' inaugurated by Cardano, Maurolycus and

Digges in the early 1550s,[6] and the replication of northern European 'distant point construction' perspective is its primary design objective.[7] The photographic image accommodates the previously established codes of representation just as the social circumstances in which these new images were and are consumed conform to pre-existing and culturally specific patterns. The apparatus is not neutral, and turning its purpose requires considerable deformation of its inherent (i.e. designed-in) capacities and capabilities.

Understanding of the ideological implications of the institution of the cinema, including its apparatus, has broadened from (comparatively) simple considerations of the ideological intentions or implications of this or that film text to include psychologically inflected discussions of the unavoidable ideo-logical effects of viewing films and, to a lesser degree, television,[8] as well as accounts and explanations of the development and implications of the entire technical apparatus and economic structure of the film and television indus-tries,[9] as we have seen in Chapter One. This case study is, in general, part of this latter project. It looks specifically at the narrower competencies – the ideas, devices, mind-sets and techniques – available to the technologists who were to develop colour film. In terms of the model, the chapter attempts to chart the course of this technology from science (as I am terming the aggre-gation of these competencies) through ideation to performance, that is the actual creation of a colour film.

'Natural' Colour

> We so often forget, for example, that when a colour film is seen projected, the colour is not in the Bazanian sense a direct ... registration of colour in the natural world. ... There is, in fact, no direct ... link between the colour of the natural world and the colour of the projected colour film – a whole technology of dyeing has intervened.[10]

The makers of *El Pueblo Vincera*, a colour film, must have been aware of the limitations placed upon them by the use of colour when filming black people. All professionals fully understand that colour films, despite continuous im-provements in performance, do not render black skin tones as easily as they do white; and that, when filming blacks, it is often necessary to augment lighting, by bouncing reflected light back into the face from a low angle, for instance, so as not to lose details. Were these stocks to offer 'a direct ... regis-tration of colour in the natural world', we could simply attribute the difficul-ties of filming black people to a natural racial disadvantage – somewhat like, say, sickle-cell anaemia. But colour film, and colour television systems, do *not* directly register the world; 'a whole technology' intervenes. As the comedian Godfrey Cambridge once hyperbolised – but only slightly – African-Americans look green on American (NTSC) television; no amount of knob-twiddling changes their colour (unless one makes the whites orange); and he for one was not surprised. The history and ideological implications of these technol-ogies, technologies created by whites which best reproduce Caucasian skin

41

tones, offer a good case study in technological agenda-setting at the stage when a technology is transformed from idea to existence.

At one level it is 'inevitable' that the bias of colour film should be the way it is. After all, according to Kodak, more than 8 billion colour negative exposures were made in the US alone in 1982, and the vast majority of them were by and of whites.[11] But the rhetoric surrounding colour film, as much in the technical and scholarly literature as in advertising and other popular accounts, implicitly denies any such partiality in favour of a stress on naturalness, realism and verisimilitude – mathematics, as it were, rather than painting. Even aware scholars slip easily into this language. Edward Branigan, for instance, in an otherwise most illuminating account of how film historians have represented the development of colour cinematography, writes of additive and subtractive photographic methods, describing both as 'natural colour processes':

> It is enough to note, without exploring details, that *natural* colour processes are usually divided into two types - additive colour systems (e.g. KinemaColor, early Technicolor and modern television) and subtractive colour systems (e.g. Technicolor, Eastman colour, and Kodachrome). ... we have considered the invention of colour with respect to the photograph (*natural* colour), but a second line of development lies closer to painting. Hand-painted daguerreotypes appeared around 1839 and hand-painted films appeared with the very first films in 1894 ... [emphasis added].[12]

A survey of colour processes written for a professional journal by an official of Eastman Kodak highlights the supposed *naturalness* of the company's subtractive systems but masks this subtle sales pitch in the language of impeccable scientific description.

> All of the [additive] systems discussed ... have resulted in a final picture being put on the screen in colour by superimposing or adding the lights of two or three primary colours. In nature, however, colours of objects are viewed by subtraction; they absorb or subtract certain component parts of the visible spectrum of white light and reflect the remainder, which the eye sees as colour.[13]

This supposed analogy between human vision and the way Eastman Kodak's colour films 'view' nature (i.e. just like we humans do) is obviously anthropomorphic and tendentious. Such language is the norm.

Discourse at a general scientific level therefore systematically denies the cultural specificity of colour film and instead suggests that the stocks, true to their scientific heritage, reflect and re-present the natural world *in a natural (i.e. human) way*. This places the development of colour squarely within that received view, theoretically legitimated by André Bazin, which argues that the entire technological development of cinema progressively seeks to possess the world mimetically. Natalie Kalmus, wife of the 'inventor' of Technicolor, Herbert Kalmus, expressed this view in 1935 when addressing a meeting of Hollywood technicians under the significant rubric 'Colour Consciousness':

> From a technical standpoint, motion pictures have been steadily tending towards a more complete realism. In the early days, pictures were a mere mechanical process of imprinting light upon film and projecting that result upon a screen. Then came the perfection of detail – more accurate sets and costumes – more perfect photography. The advent of sound brought increased realism through the auditory senses. The last step, colour, with the addition of the chromatic sensations completed the process. Now motion pictures are able to duplicate faithfully all the auditory and visual sensations. This enhanced realism enables us to portray life and nature as it really is, and in this respect we have made definite strides forward.[14]

Within this claim of general faithful duplication, 'flesh' always comes to mean Caucasian skin tones.[15] Only in the mid-50s does a degree of what might be called sophistication begin to creep into the professional scientific discourse, for example: 'Flesh-colour, even of the so-called "white" races, varies from light pink or almost white to various shades of tan and brown according to the type of skin and the amount of sunburn ...'[16] However, elsewhere in the standard work just quoted, 'flesh' ranks between 'yellow' and 'sand' or is proximate to 'peach' and 'white'.[17]

It is no wonder that the cultural assumptions of those concerned with the development and applications of colour film are those of the society at large. Natalie Kalmus, for instance, had these unsurprising things to say about 'black' and 'white':

> Black is no colour, but the absorption of all colour. It has a distinctly negative and destructive aspect. Black instinctively recalls night, fear, darkness, crime. It suggests funerals, mourning. It is impenetrable, comfortless, secretive. It flies at the masthead of the pirate's ship. Our language is replete with references to this frightful power of black – black art, black despair, blackguard, blackmail, black hand, the black hole of Calcutta, black death (the devastating plague of medieval Europe), black list, black-hearted etc. ... White represents purity, cleanliness, peace and marriage. Its introduction into a colour sublimates that colour. For example, the red of love becomes more refined and idealistic as white transforms the red to pink. White uplifts and ennobles, while black lowers and renders more base and evil any colour.[18]

It is no sin that Kalmus and her peers were less sophisticated than say, Wittgenstein (or Eisenstein) about colour. The sin is that they claimed, both in practice and theory, to be doing what came naturally, rather than recognising the cultural influences that led them, through complex optics and chemistry, to what was (and remains) a highly mediated, ideologically charged analogue of the natural world of colour.

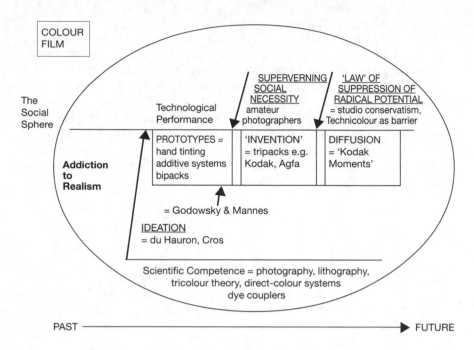

PAST ——————————————————————————————▶ FUTURE

I am using the case of colour film to illustrate the early phases of the model, the transformation from science to technology through the ideation phase. The competencies involved in the ground of science include: the technology of photography; the colour printing techniques of lithography; photographic systems that captured directly the wave characteristics of colour; the chemicals – dye couplers – that stain photographic materials; and the theory of primary colours, specifically the trichromatic concept that three primary colours can be combined together or subtracted from each other to produce a full range of colours.

Additive and subtractive systems were developed for colour photography in the last quarter of the 19th century by researchers such as du Hauron and Cros. The idea of producing a fully chromatically sensitive film using the three basic colours in some chemical fashion on a single celluloid base, a tripack, occurred to various workers in the years after World War I. However, Godowsky and Mannes, two independent amateur chemists eventually recruited by Eastman Kodak, were the first to perfect a dye-coupler system to do this. This is the ideation phase. It produces prototype additive colour motion-picture systems using complex cameras and projectors with colour filters as well as bipack two-colour systems such as that used by Technicolor in the 20s before the tripack emerges as the 'invention': that is, the innovation that will be widely diffused.

I am concerned in this case with these early phases of development, but we can note that, within our general cultural addiction to realistic modes of representation, it is the market for amateur film which primarily sustains the research effort of the ideation phase and therefore constitutes the supervening necessity for colour stocks. Moving further on in the model, it is the conservatism of the studios hiding behind Technicolor's near monopoly and Kodak's concern to protect its monochrome amateur markets which work as constraints to suppress the diffusion of the tripack after its 'invention'.

Reproducing Colour

I want to begin by suggesting that the ideologically charged, cultural assumptions about the nature of colour condition and affect the work of the people involved in the development of colour film and lie behind and beneath what they accomplished. One can exempt from this only one line of inquiry: that which produced systems designed to capture information about colour in the form of wave-length data – what might be termed direct colour systems.

Colours vary by wave formation and there are two methods currently available for capturing this information directly onto a photographic plate – that is, without any chemical dyeing or electronic technologies intervening. In one, microdispersion developed by F. W. Lanchester in 1895, a coarse grating, with some 300 slits per inch, is interposed within the body of the camera between the taking lens and the film. The grating breaks up the light, which is then collected by a second lens and passed through a narrow angled prism. Lenses on either side of the prism, the third and fourth needed by the system, focus the image of the slits (turned by the prism into spectra) on to the photographic plate. By these means the image is broken down into its constituent colour elements – dominant wavelength, chroma, luminance and value – which are then recorded on the plate. After development the plate can be viewed by reversing the light path through the system so that the taking lens becomes a projection lens, and all of the original chromaticities and intensities are re-created.[19]

The other direct method was developed in 1891 by Gabriel Lippmann, professor of physics at the Sorbonne from 1878 and a Nobel laureate in 1908. It was a Lippman 'photochrome' made in the summer of 1893 by the Lumière brothers which ranks as the first colour portrait. Unlike the micro-dispersion method, the Lippmann system does not require a special camera, only a modified plate holder. It depends on an emulsion of extremely fine grain, wherein the individual photosensitive granules are physically shorter than the colour wavelengths that are to be recorded. The plate is placed in the camera with the emulsion side away from the lens. Upon exposure, Lippmann poured a film of pure mercury against the emulsion, thus turning it into a mirror. The light waves of the image are reflected in the mercury back against the incoming waves and the interference pattern thereby caused is recorded on the plate. This three-dimensional pattern of stationary waves in the emulsion can then be developed and contains all the information of the chromaticities and intensities of the original colours. The image can be re-produced by using reflected light passed through the plate.[20]

Photochromes are obsolete and never enjoyed any degree of popularity. (However, the basic idea of recording image data as an interference pattern on a photographic plate and reconstructing the image by passing light through the plate is the basis of all holographic techniques. It is therefore, as we shall see in Chapter Five, still too soon to draw the line under Lippmann's contribution to the technologies of seeing.) But for the purposes of colour photography, the fine grain required by photochromes to record accurately all the colour data means emulsions so slow as apparently to require several minutes of exposure even in sunlight; and the images can be viewed only by carefully positioning the eye at a precise angle, otherwise no colour can be seen at all. Similar difficulties attach to the microdispersion method. The special camera is bulky and the additional optics, as well as the fine grain, necessitate strong illumination and long exposures. However real or otherwise these disadvantages are,[21] the direct systems do seem to require considerable light and certainly yield no prints.

There was no supervening necessity to ensure the diffusion of these techniques; in effect, not enough demand for such 'scientific' direct colour pictures to overcome the difficulties involved in making such images. For all that photochromes record photographically the physical parameters of the original spectral phenomena, the human eye/brain mechanism does not require such a degree of fidelity since it normally simplifies the colour information it processes. What might be termed 'indirect' artificial renditions of colour, it turns out, need not represent reality as faithfully as direct methods do. Filters and dyes are psychologically effective, although the abandoned direct processes remain as the standard by which the limitations of the more than a hundred filter and dye-based indirect systems must be measured.

The concept of primary colours was understood from the first years of the 17th century and, by 1722 at the latest, it was clear that three mezzo-tinted copper plates, one blue, one red and one yellow, would produce, when superimposed, a full colour plate. The laborious handwork on stone this system required was superseded by lithography, another three-colour process introduced commercially in 1812. In 1861 the great English physicist Clerk Maxwell, while discoursing on the nature of human colour perception, offered a suggestion as to how such a system might work with photography:

Let it be required to ascertain the colours of a landscape by means of impressions taken on a preparation equally sensitive to rays of every colour. Let a plate of red glass be placed before the camera, and an impression taken. The positive of this will be transparent wherever the red light has been abundant in the landscape, and opaque where it has been wanting. Let it now be put in a magic lantern with the red glass, and a red picture will be thrown on the screen. Let this operation be repeated with a green and a violet glass, and by means of three magic lanterns let the three images be superimposed on the screen. The colour on any point on the screen will depend on that of the corresponding point of the landscape, and by properly adjusting the intensities of the lights, etc., a complete copy of the landscape, as far as visible colour is concerned, will be thrown on the screen.[22]

The actual demonstration of such a photographic method was first made in 1873 by Louis Ducos du Hauron (whom we have already met as the man who patented but did not build a movie system). He patented a colour camera that exposed three images behind three coloured filters at the same instant.

The three-colour method is the basis for all current colour reproductive methods, photographic and electronic, and at first it might seem as if it agrees well with the physiology of the human eye.[23] By 1807, Thomas Young had established that the cones of the retina, those photoreceptors sensitive to colour, were of three types, the ρ (responsive to red – orange – yellow), the γ (responsive to orange – yellow – green - blue/green) and the β (responsive to blue/green – blue – violet). If Maxwell's filters, or any dyes used in a photographic process, triggered only one of these cone-types as appropriate, then the pattern of stimulation caused by viewing the reproduction would exactly agree with the original stimulus – as occurs in Professor Lippmann's images, for instance.

Unfortunately no filter can be found which will activate only the γ-cones. Wherever green appears there will be an excess of β- and ρ-cone stimulus that will render greens paler and, although scarcely noticeable in the reds and blues, will also cause whites to acquire a magenta tinge. Increasing the intensity of the red and blue lights or dyes restores the white but at the cost of distortion in the relative chromaticities and intensities – which, as it happens, is psychologically (or, perhaps better, ideologically) less offensive than producing off-whites. And here is opened a whole can of coloured worms, especially close (chromatically speaking) to Caucasian skin tones.

This is not the place in which to outline the range of choices facing those chemists and physicists whose job it is to produce colour-sensitive photographic materials and electronic systems. Suffice it only to point out that with trichromatic systems (contemporary colour systems, that is) the opportunities for choice and the need for design decisions are boundless; that is why one colour film or colour television system is easily distinguished from another and none, it can fairly be claimed, is perfectly mimetic.

Colour in Motion
From the beginning, motion picture films were hand-coloured and were very often, if not most of the time, printed on tinted stocks. With the introduction of sound, tinting at the development stage was abandoned because the process interfered with the optical soundtrack. Kodak responded by introducing a range of seventeen tinted Sonochrome positive stocks that did not affect the audio track. However, monochrome movies, tinted or not, were so successful in the market that the search for an effective colour system was never in the forefront of Hollywood's mind. The supervening social necessity that carried research and development on colour forward was, in general, the on-going cultural addiction to realism and, more specifically, the need for new product lines in the amateur market; although, here too, the success of monochrome inhibited the search for colour.

47

Kinemacolour, the earliest movie system to exploit the Maxwell additive approach, was in commercial operation by 1909. It was a two-colour sequential process in which camera (and projector) alternatively exposed frames through revolving filters disks, at an increased rate of thirty-two frames per second. The disks contained two filters, one cyan/blue, the other red/orange.[24] The Dowager Empress of Russia, after watching at Buckingham Palace the Kinemacolour film of George V's Delhi Durbar, pronounced that it 'gives one the impression of having seen it all in reality'.[25]

Other subsequent additive systems rang the changes on the basic method of superimposing discretely tinted images. These included squeezing the images on to one 35mm frame or, in a significant development, splitting the image so that it fell through a green or red filter on to two separate film strips. Apart from registration difficulties, the comparative darkness of the blue filter translated into a brightness flicker in the sequential variants of this approach, and there was always a tendency, whatever system was used, towards colour fringing – i.e., chromaticities did not agree exactly with the outlines of objects but bled. Eventually these additive processes would encompass three colour filters rather than two, as many as four filtered images per frame and, always, extremely complex cameras and projectors. Although the last variant was proposed as late as 1950, additive colour reproduction never took hold in the cinema. Kalmus, of Technicolor, in describing what drove him from additive to subtractive processes, graphically illustrates why:

> During one terrible night in Buffalo, I decided that such special attachments on the projector required an operator who was a cross between a college professor and an acrobat, a phrase which I have since heard repeated many times. Technicolor then and there abandoned additive processes and special attachments on the projector.[26]

So it was that, after six years of effort, Kalmus, the pioneer of viable movie colour, quit the search for additive solutions in 1922.

The alternative processes rely on a series of separate trichromatically filtered black-and-white images, but instead of remaining discrete, each image is dyed and then superimposed – as in lithography – upon the others to create the full-colour picture. Again, Ducos du Hauron and, independently, Charles Cros, by 1868/9, were using chemicals such as coralinne and chlorophyll to dye discrete plates to create such full colour images. Obviously a subtractive system could in theory produce a coloured film that would simply be threaded through a standard projector.[27]

The major problem lay in the difficulty of dyeing the negatives with three colours. The earliest solution to the problem involved utilising a line of techniques developed to produce photogravure systems. These relied on the fact that gelatin swelled during development and swelled more if further exposed. Photographic printing using printers' ink was first experimentally demonstrated in 1855 and an 'imbibing' – or relief image – process for colour, 'collotyping', was introduced in 1874.[28] In a colour collotype, the gelatin of the negative swells up or becomes thinner in proportion to the intensity of the exposure, allowing a colour developing procedure in which the colour dye solution adheres to the raised parts. The more exposed the gelatin the more it imbibes the liquid dye intensifying the hue. Three sequential imbibings of primary colour dyes could create a full trichromatic subtractive image on one gelatin base. This dyed image is readily copied so that many prints can be run off, although doing this is actually complex and craft-like.

It was to this well-established if tricky technique that Kalmus turned when he abandoned the coloured filters of additive colour. The first Technicolor subtractive process used two negatives (one sensitive to the red–yellow range, another to the green–blue) cemented back-to-back. In a 1928 refinement, Kalmus managed to get them onto the same celluloid base – a 'bipack'. But this did not produce a fully chromatic image and the third negative needed to accomplish this could not be also cemented in place. To solve the problem, Kalmus returned to a special beam-splitter camera, of a design first introduced in 1918, which used two negatives. By 1932 the Technicolor process involved not just stock and developing techniques, but also this special camera, which exposed the blue–red bipack film and, simultaneously, a separate green negative. Imbibing then produced a three-colour master.

The system, in all its various forms, privileged the lab, because that was where the colour image – for all that it was supposedly bound to represent colours in the real world – was, in effect, created. Although neither the special camera not the superiority of Technicolor's imbibing technique were of Kalmus's devising, they enabled him to demand and obtain considerable control over films shot with this process. He had perfected the most effective exploitation of known methods. Exceptional craft in the laboratory, as much as any other factor, became the basis of Technicolor's hegemony over cinema colour. The close control exercised by Kalmus's 'colour consultants' – often over the resistance of studio technicians who were under no illusion as to Technicolor's 'naturalness' – limited the circumstances in which the film was exposed. Only Technicolor's technicians were allowed to operate the camera. Only sets, costumes and lighting designs to which Technicolor best responded were allowed. The result was that the stock established its own reference system consistent, not with nature, but only with itself; exactly the consistency required, according to Tolkien, in any fairy-tale world.

By the late 40s, Technicolor's hegemony, based as it was on unoriginal processes, brought in train a host of patent and anti-trust problems.[29] Slowly its hold was broken. In part this related paradoxically to Technicolor's essential strength, the quality arising from its careful craft. It had only three laboratories - in Hollywood, New Jersey and London - and it simply could not handle the post-war rising tide of colour features. By 1948 it was reportedly demanding nine months' lead-time on principle photography, and printing schedules were being planned three years in advance.[30] As a result, by 1953 the camera and special negative stocks had been abandoned. Technicolor became what it remains today, essentially only a multinational chain of laboratories bringing special skills to Eastman Kodak materials, and Kalmus's multi-negative process, for all its early dominance, turned out to be nothing but the last of the prototypes of colour cinematography.

Eastman Kodak had been rigorously pursuing colour for decades but had reached dead-ends. The original – additive – Kodachrome was introduced in 1913 and in 1916 was adapted for movies by use of a beam-splitter camera. It was no more successful than the other additive systems of the day. In 1928 Kodak began to manufacture a film it named Kodacolor. This was a lenticular 16mm stock which Kodak produced under licence from its French developers. Twenty years before, Gabriel Lippmann had envisioned a film stock that had, in effect, a myriad of tiny lenses embedded in the emulsion – a monochrome extension, in some sense, of his previous direct colour system – which would allow for normal viewing. The following year, that is, in 1909, Rudolph Berthon thought to place a three-colour filter before such a film, and by 1923 a successful demonstration of a colour lenticular process was given in Paris. The method produced prints of great delicacy, but attempts by Kodak, Paramount and the French to manufacture a viable 35mm version of a lenticular stock were fruitless – like the early Technicolor, just another prototype. Anyway, by that time, the mid-30s, Kodak was ready with the 'invention', a new, easy-to-use subtractive film which it called Kodachrome.[31]

The chemistry that would enable subtraction to take place on a single negative was understood in the same year Berthon began developing the lenticular stock. Rudolph Fischer and his assistant Johann Siegrist noticed that parahenylendamine, a photographic developer, produced oxidisations as it worked on the silver halides of a black-and-white film. It 'coupled' with the emulsion to form a colour, in effect making an insoluble dye.[32] Fischer patented the idea of such 'colour-formers' or 'dye-couplers' in 1912 and publicised a growing list of compound substances, each of which produced a different colour, in a series of patents and reports in the British, French, German and American technical press before World War I.[33] Other workers in the early 20s added to the number of known couplers, but it was two young American amateur chemists (and professional musicians) who were to create the first practical application of Fischer's breakthrough.

In 1924 Leopold Godowsky Jr. and Leopold Mannes patented a reversal film stock where two emulsions were placed on a single base, the lower one faster and sensitised to red, the upper one slower and sensitised to green – blue/green.[34] Clearly, the combination of dye-couplers and multilayer variable-speed emulsions had the potential of producing, on one base, an integral full colour image with the trichromatic filters and all the necessary dyes chemically 'built in', as it were. By 1930 Godowsky and Mannes, working privately, still remained a step ahead of the industrial laboratories. At this point, Kodak had the good sense to hire them, and they moved out of various hotel rooms and the bathrooms of their parents' New York apartments to Rochester. By 1933 they had perfected a bipack reversal system for 16mm use; then on 15 April 1935, Kodak offered a new Kodachrome amateur movie stock, a 'tripack' of the sort implied by Cros's vision nearly seventy years earlier and first built experimentally by Ducos du Hauron in 1897. What Godowsky and Mannes had finally given Kodak was a marketable tripack, a 'monopack'. The ideation and 'invention' phases for colour film were over.

For the first time, a colour stock that required no special cameras was commercially available. Kodak sold the film in a form that required the couplers be added, not to the emulsion, but during the development process. This created a situation as privileged as the one into which Kalmus had steered Technicolor; anybody could *expose* Kodachrome, but only Kodak could *develop* it. It was not entirely inappropriate that Kodachrome's 'inventors' were known in the Kodak Research Laboratory as 'God and Man'. They had not only broken through into a new market for amateur colour photography with a reliable product, one step in front of rivals like Dr Bela Gaspar whose tripack Gasparcolour had been announced in 1934,[35] but in so doing they had also created a virtual processing monopoly. (The German company Agfa also produced a comparable stock at the same time but with the couplers *built into* the film so that it could be developed anywhere.)

One can note that this careful control of the market allowed Eastman Kodak to protect its monochrome business. At first the stock was only available for amateur movie-makers, with whom I deal in the next chapter. It was only slowly introduced into the amateur stills market, allowing monochrome to survive for decades after World War II. This is, once again, a good example of the suppression of radical potential at work.

However, Kodak did not just protect its own business. Despite the fact that, unlike lenticular stock, Kodachrome could be manufactured in the 35mm format and did not require special cameras, the company did not produce a movie stock. So there is a point to be made in this connection about Hollywood's essential conservatism, a theme to which I will return in subsequent chapters. There is no doubt that Kodak would not have demanded from the studios the level of control Kalmus was exercising – for one thing, the tripack did not need a special patented camera – but, nevertheless, Kodachrome did not conquer Hollywood.

As is usually the case, the new technology was contained and its disruptive potential lessened. The 'law' was at work. For the studios, colour was expensive, adding about 30 per cent to production costs during the 30s.[36] Since black-and-white still filled the theatres, there was no pressing commercial reason to expand colour film production. Anyway, cheaper colour techniques, like cheaper sound recording techniques, as we will see in Chapter Three, were not necessarily an advantage. Technicolor, because of its expense and the controlled way it was used, constituted a very effective barrier against outsiders. Moreover, what little colour production had taken place, comparatively speaking, had served to make Technicolor an essential part, almost a trade-mark element, of the Hollywood product. Why lose that for a more ubiquitous colour reproductive system? Remember, this is an industry which had already totally retooled for sound. It was happy to contain the potential disruption of colour by continuing to use an antiquated and complicated technology.

For Kodak, breaking Kalmus's hold on the studios was not worth the comparatively paltry pickings the motion picture market represented. For instance, by 1948 Kodak's net sales were some twenty times greater than Technicolor's, and included, of course, all Hollywood's black-and-white

51

film.[37] Anyway, to pick up a share of that business, Eastman had come to a licence accommodation with Kalmus which gave Technicolor access to some Kodak monopack patents. With these, Technicolor abandoned its patented cameras but not its hold on Hollywood. Also a few films were shot on Kodak colour stock, the first being *Thunderhead* in 1942. The result was to bring these various forces into a rough balance so that, '*in time*, Eastman colour negative film ... replaced the need for the bulky three-strip camera used by Technicolor' (emphasis added).[38] It is the 'in time' which demonstrates that the 'law' of the suppression of radical potential was in operation.

This is then a good example of how suppression operates. The essential element of the new technology is adopted by the existing dominant player; in this case Technicolor, the dominant player in 35mm colour film, gets the monopack. The owner of the new technology gets an enormous new market – amateur colour photography and, to a very much lesser extent, amateur 16mm movie-making – but is bought off in the secondary area of 35mm movie production via a patent licence agreement with the existing dominant player and the odd, virtually experimental, production. Finally, the end-user, the movie industry, gets a measure of stability and continuity as well as the crucially important protection afforded by an inaccessible and distinctive technology. Behind these arrangements, the technological changeover occurs which sees, over the two decades from the mid-30s to the mid-50s, Technicolor reduced to a film processing company but not destroyed while Hollywood moves almost entirely to colour production and Kodak maintains and, indeed, consolidates its leading position as a film stock manufacturer despite the eventual decline in black-and-white production.

But I am here concerned primarily with the deep-seated cultural factors conditioning the development of stocks such as Kodachrome, so let us now return to the main issue – cultural determinants in the development of colour films such a Kodakchrome.

The Meaning of Colour
Because these solutions all produced approximations and involved trade-offs in colour responsiveness, grain and overall sensitivity, that was not the end of the matter. The monopack – that is, the tripack subtractive film – has undergone immense development since Godowsky and Mann's day. Agfa introduced a colour-negative film just before World War II. Kodak marketed Ektachrome, a tripack with built-in couplers which could be developed at home. Edwin Land adapted his instant monochrome system to Polacolor in 1962. In general, all these film stocks gained steadily over the years in both sensitivity (with no concomitant increase in grain) and overall responsiveness.

These changes had a considerable effect on the production process. I have presented this history as a locus of choice and decision on the part of the chemists involved and their employers, but the colour image depends, as Technicolor's insistence on control of the filmic event reveals, on more than just the stock. The image can be altered within the parameters of the film during processing, although with colour until very recently these options were much reduced. There are other major factors involved. Technicolor's move on to the studio floor was motivated as much by a desire to maintain absolute control over lighting as to prohibit outsiders from loading the cameras. (This was done ostensibly to protect the patent, but since that was a matter of public record, other factors must have been at work. Technicolor's corporate culture made something of a fetish of secrecy.) When coupled with the existing power of the laboratory, as well as control over sets, costume and make-up, the crucial command of lighting ensured the consistency of Technicolor's performance, especially as sets, costumes and make-up could also be bent to highlight the process's most responsive aspects.

Natural and man-made 'white' unfiltered lights are actually coloured. They range from, say, the blue of a northern sky through sunlight, to projection bulbs and the comparative red of ordinary incandescent household lamps. (As conventionally measured in degrees Kelvin, these examples run from 7,500 for the northern sky to 2,800 for the household lamp.) With monochrome film, the colour of the illumination is significant but not critical. With colour film, of course, it assumes a far greater moment. The problem is that the colour of the light will affect the way in which Caucasian skin is represented. Films are therefore differently formatted for different lighting conditions – indoor and artificial versus outdoor and natural being the commonest division – so that the chemistry of the stock compensates for the colour of the light and 'white' flesh tones remain constant.

After World War I, film lighting had settled its own artificial code, mixing, in the interests of maintaining a largely realist convention, a number of theatrical systems; basic flat lighting, lighting for effects and spotlighting. Peter Baxter persuasively argues that as electricity was introduced into the studios in the years before that war, there was a desire to emulate the most advanced stage techniques: 'the cinema was moving in the same direction as commercial American theatre, and a few paces behind it.'[39] The combination of techniques resulted in the 'three-point' (i.e., keylight, fill-light and backlight) overhead system – with almost no floor-level sources except for special effects – that is still in use today. For Baxter, this application of the electric light expresses the dominant ideological assumptions of the studios in creating a style that operates by 'revelation and expression'.[40]

Monochrome stocks became ever more sensitive until, in the late 30s, general lighting levels could be reduced by 70 per cent. The studios were now so dim, comparatively speaking, that cinematographers began to use photoelectric light meters to ensure proper exposure, something the mysterium of the craft did not previously allow.[41] A sequence of responses, ostensibly occasioned by changes in technology (sound as well as colour), can be traced in lighting, set and costume design and make-up.

These changes are more complex than a simple technological progression suggests, since they actually reflect the forces at work within the organisation of the industry and the social positioning of Hollywood, as well as the underlying thrust towards an ever more transparent mode of representation. In short, these technological developments were positioned as a prophylactic

53

against widespread film-making in the society. Movie production became, like newspaper production a hundred years earlier, more and more capital-intensive and therefore less and less accessible. This is the trajectory, a common one in the histories of media technologies, which the cinema traces. Once established behind a 'high-tech' bastion of more complex lighting and the rest, then cheaper monopack colour systems could slowly come on stream. It is possible for industry insiders like Natalie Kalmus and for scholars to argue that this reflects a drive for realism, which the scholars at least would acknowledge as ideologically significant; but the drive is just as much or more conditioned by industrial protectionism.

Indeed, one can make an argument that colour, despite what Technicolor claimed, was in no way a move towards greater mimesis. Colour was more than unrealistic and not just in the sense of being a highly manufactured approximation of the real world. It is very significant that it was not used, as Ed Buscombe points out,[42] in those sorts of movies that at first sight might have been thought to benefit most from additional 'realism' – social dramas in the genres of war and crime films (insofar as these were 'realistic') or newsreels and documentaries. (It should not be objected that the colour stocks were too slow for non-fiction, since much of it was shot outdoors and set-up. Colour newsreels were certainly possible and could have appeared much earlier than they did.) Instead, the first trichromatic Technicolor film was Disney's Oscar-winning cartoon *Flowers and Trees*. Douglas Fairbanks, star of the bichromatic Technicolor feature *The Pirate*, complained that colour could distract the eye, confuse the action, and, presumably worst of all, 'take attention from acting and facial expression'.[43] Buscombe argues that colour came to denote luxury, spectacle or fantasy, and a celebration of its own technological mastery. Thus, Kansas is black and white; Oz is technicolored. So much did colour come to signify a lack of serious intent that a Pathé producer was able to announce in 1947: 'The French don't go in for musicals or colour.'[44] This statement has further ideological import as it is a salvo in what Dudley Andrews calls the 'colour cold war'.

After the real war, World War II, the differences between the German Agfacolour and the American colour films assumed an overt ideological significance when the Russians adopted, or rather captured, the former. Agfacolour (originally a product of the Nazi era) became a 'socialist' stock; it had paler colours, muted edges and an increased sensitivity to pastels. This was in contrast to Technicolor, which was 'purer than reality, needing strong artificial light, aggressive, almost whorish'. These are the terms, Dudley Andrews suggests, in which the French perceived the ideological differences in this 'colour cold war' of the late 40s.[45] Andrews makes France the battleground of this conflict. After World War II, the French, lacking a domestic subtractive system, were faced with choosing between domestic additive (and therefore obsolete) methods, including a revived lenticular stock, or importing foreign technology. The domestic systems failed and the French chose Agfacolour, albeit disguised in a politically acceptable form because obtained from Agfa's pre-war Belgian partners, Gaevert. Technicolor, by this account, lost out in France in part because of French ambivalence about *le défi Américain* – 'a desire for, and a loathing of, American technology', in Andrews' phrase.

A confusion therefore exists about the signification of colour in the Hollywood film, a confusion that simultaneously deems colour real and fantastic; there is also a certain cognitive dissonance in the professional discourse. Even Natalie Kalmus realised that despite motion pictures' faithful duplication of 'all the auditory and visual sensations', there is a distinction between 'natural colours and lights' and 'man-made colours and artificial lights'.[46] It is, though, a distinction she and her fellow workers devoted their lives to ignoring.

'Pleasing Flesh Tones'

If colour has meaning, no colour has more meaning than skin colour: 'perhaps the most important single factor in dramatic cinematography is the relation between the colour sensitivity of an emulsion and the reproduction of pleasing flesh tones.'[47] But not all flesh tones are equally pleasing and in the chemistry of colour film not all can be equally readily accommodated. The failure to find a direct, that is unmanipulated, colour system requires not only that chemical manipulation take place; it allows such manipulation to accommodate the cultural prejudices of the users. It is even possible to make, by careful chemistry, already pleasing (by which we may understand Caucasian) flesh tones more pleasing than they are in nature. However, that chemistry *allows* this is, of course, no proof that such manipulation actually went – and goes – on.

The history of the development of colour film with its numerous different 'brands', its various distinct systems of reproduction, reveals that colour photography is not bound to be 'faithful' to the natural world. Choices are made in the development and production of photographic materials. That much is incontrovertible. It is also clear that there are considerable difficulties in representing Caucasian skin tones because of the way in which the colour receptor system in the human eye operates. And, finally, that colours have symbolic meanings and that we are politically and culturally sensitive to human skin tones goes without saying. But I want to demonstrate how these last prejudices inform the research and development in the photographic materials industry. Given the scientific thrust towards a depersonalised discourse of objectivity, even trace elements of how these forces might effect the research agenda during the ideation phase are hard to find. However, there is an instance in the technical literature when these normally unspoken prejudices begin to surface.

I want to suggest that this technical paper is valuable not only in its own terms as a history of the beginnings of the post-war version of the world's dominant amateur still film but also as a proof of my contention that the social sphere invades the laboratory and conditions the technological performance of those who work there.

Kodachrome was subject to constant development in the Kodak Research Laboratories. It was during the work after World War II, which was to lead eventually to Kodachrome II, that determining which prejudices about skin

55

colour might be in play in the society became an overt agenda item for the researchers rather than just an unstated area of assumption. In a report on this research, written in 1951 for the *Journal of the SMPTE*, David MacAdam of Eastman Kodak describes the following experiment:

> Series of color prints have been made from well-exposed colour separation negatives of several typical scenes. The prints of each of these differ in tone reproduction, balance and in other ways subject to controlled variation. These series have been presented to numerous judges, and their judgments have been compared with results of measurements of various colours in the prints.

Central to this positivist social science enterprise was a series of prints of a portrait of 'a young lady' which exhibited

> variations of balance from too red or yellow to too blue, and from too green to too pink. These prints were submitted to a number of judges who were asked to accept or reject each on the basis of colour alone. ... Optimum reproduction of skin colour is not 'exact' reproduction. ... 'exact reproduction' is rejected almost unanimously as 'beefy'. On the other hand, when the print of highest acceptance is masked and compared with the original subject, it seems quite pale. ...
>
> The discrepancy between 'exact' reproduction and preferred reproduction is partly due to distortions inherent in the process, such that a certain discrepancy of a particular colour is necessary to permit the best over-all reproduction of all colours in the picture.
>
> Similar results have been obtained with other colours. The directions and amounts of difference between exact reproduction and optimum reproduction are different for every colour tested.[48]

Kodak, faced with the physical inevitability of distortion, here establishes the potential superiority of its products to the real world. The subject of the photograph can be made to have skin tones more pleasing than she has in reality. Exact reproduction, a supposed goal of the photographic and cinematographic project, takes second place to inexact, culturally determined, 'optimum' reproduction. Caucasian skin tones are not to be rendered as they are, but rather as they are preferred – a white shade of white. The results of such social investigations, as well as the growing understanding of the physics of colour, the physiology of perception, and the chemistry of dyes and films, were being translated into ever more culturally determined products.

All this is not to suggest some crude conspiracy on the part of the industrial chemists or physicists responsible for the colour of the moving image, much less to single out the Kodak researchers who produced Kodachrome II. My supposition is that these sorts of considerations and, indeed, experiments have taken place constantly in every film processing laboratory in the world. Why else would Fujicolor, for instance, emerge as less 'beefy' than Western stocks? I would also suggest that the same considerations

56

have affected the development of colour television systems. The most transmitted early image on British colour television screens was a test card that focused on a portrait of a young white child.

All the above Kodak account does is to draw attention to this normally hidden dimension of technological development during the ideation phase. It points up the existence of choices in the development of these processes and suggests that in situations of choice, consciously or unconsciously, cultural determinants will operate – as much in the scientific environment of a research laboratory as anywhere. The Kodak experiment cited above speaks eloquently to how research is always redolent of a specific culture. In this case, the results produce film stocks which are not readily manipulated to give good black skin tones. In the case of Kodachrome II the manipulation actually worsens the stock's ability so to do.

That this should warrant attention is only the result of the operations of media, technology and, especially, media technology in the culture. These operations, in a sense hidden because transparent, conform perfectly to Barthes's ineffable ideology. In the case of colour film so disguised are these assumptions that it is widely assumed that Western systems of colour reproduction can supposedly be used as tools against themselves, as if a whole technology of dyeing had not intervened.

The next phase of the model is concerned with the transformation from innovation ('invention') to wide diffusion and importance of social necessity as a transformative agent. This is well illustrated by the history of 16mm film.

Chapter 3: The Case of 16mm Film

From Home Movies to *Cinéma Vérité:*
Looking for a Need

The long suppression of 16mm between the 20s and the 50s and the final diffusion of the gauge between the 50s and the 70s highlights the power of 'necessity' in the process gauge of technological development and change. The 16mm was marketed in 1923, yet the 16mm era does not really begin for another three decades. The reasons for this delay speak to the need for Braudelian accelerators – supervening necessities in my language – in this process. The problem with 16mm was that it was created for a market which never really blossomed – amateur cinematography. And those who could have created an alternative market for the gauge, documentary film-makers for instance, chose for various reasons to ignore its potential. It was only the necessities first of military education and entertainment in World War II and then television news in the 50s which turned the situation around.

The Standard of the Art: Edison's Strategy

It can be argued that the entire development of Hollywood technology turns on the question of 'standards' and that these, when designated as 'professional', operate as a form of suppression. Film stocks offer a particularly clear example of how this works. As far as the industry was concerned 35mm was the standard. Everything else narrower, including 16mm, was 'sub standard' or 'sub calibre' and therefore ignored.

The basic tendency in movie technology was to opt for complexity and expense, creating *de facto* barriers to entry. Not anybody could become a 'professional' film-maker. These technological barriers were institutionalised by the work of the standards committee of the Society of Motion Picture [and Television] Engineers (SMP[T]E) which, to this day, controls (or attempts to control) technological impact by previewing various technical options. Indeed, the perceived need to establish standards was the society's initial *raison d'être*. At the incorporation meeting in Washington, DC, on 24 July 1916, Henry Hubbard, the secretary of the National Bureau of Standards, spoke on the desirability of standards in the industry.[1] He began by saying, 'Your appreciation of standardisation is evident since you give it first place on your programme.'[2]

In terms of the fundamentals of cinematography, two factors were in play at the outset – the use of photographic film formatted in a strip and the size of the photographic image on that strip which in turn dictated the strip's width. As we have seen in Chapter One, prior to his encounter with Marey at the Paris exposition of 1889, Edison was thinking photographs on cylinders – as in his phonograph; after, he was thinking Marey-esque film strips with sprockets.[3] He was then confirmed in this orientation by the communication from Friese-Greene. (He might have said that 'Genius was 1 per cent inspiration and 99 per cent perspiration' but in the case of the Kinetoscope it would have been better if had adjusted the percentages to take account of his reliance on others.)

As to gauge, 35mm arose from the natural (as it were) inclination of early researchers to work with film strips in culturally familiar widths. In Britain and America this meant $\frac{1}{2}$", $\frac{3}{4}$", 1" or $1\frac{1}{2}$". Edison, tendentiously but all too typically in the first person, recorded that he had found $\frac{1}{2}$" wide images were too grainy; but it is likely that Dickson had simply assumed this to be the case after experimenting with a $\frac{3}{4}$" (19mm) strip.[4] The 1889 Kinetograph perforator-device used $\frac{3}{4}$" film[5] as did the first peep-hole viewing machines of May 1891.[6] But because $\frac{3}{4}$" was too fragile, $1\frac{1}{2}$" was also tried and in use as late as the public demonstration of the peep-hole viewer in Brooklyn in May 1893.[7] Within the year, though, with the start of commercial production of Kinetoscopes, the gauge was 1"; that is, initially, an image size of 1" between the sprocket holes and a depth of $\frac{3}{4}$" yielding a width of 35mm overall (including sprocket holes).

As we have seen in Chapter One, what is significant here is the way in which received history tends to iron out these uncertainties in the lab and thereby, in effect, 'naturalises' 35mm. It becomes inevitable and in some sense 'natural' – the standard. And, because it is the standard, any alternative technological proposals and solutions are sidetracked, ignored or actively suppressed – in fact, they are rendered 'sub-standard'.

Nevertheless, as we have seen, other standards were possible, and, indeed, initially desirable in large theatrical situations. There is no question here of the Edison team using 35mm because of the need to project a large image in a theatre. That possibility had not occurred to him nor to any of his people. The lab was working on a peep-show device, the Kinetoscope, and Dickson himself had after all apparently begun with $\frac{3}{4}$". Conversely large-screen projection had not suggested itself to Marey although he was using $3\frac{1}{2}$" (90mm) in 1888. The Chronophotographe of 1893 had used $2\frac{3}{8}$" (60mm). It seems clear that, before the introduction of the cinématographe, width was not determined by projection needs. Therefore, 35mm is not a product of theatrical screening requirements.

After the projection principle was established by the Lumières, others immediately began to exploit wider gauges. Gaumont tried 60mm in his first cinematographic apparatus in 1896.[8] As we have seen in Chapter One, Edison's most serious rival, the Mutascope/Biograph, used 70mm both to avoid patent trouble and to maximise a large image. Nevertheless, 35mm, which had not been designed specifically for theatrical exhibition, prevailed despite the greater suitability of these other wider stocks for this purpose. The adoption of 35mm as 'the standard of the art' has less to do with utility than with unexamined cultural prejudice – the elegant combination of an Anglo-Saxon inch with 35 Gallic millemetres – as well

59

as Edison's alliance with Eastman, a business arrangement which had the effect of protecting a patent which was grounded on somewhat unsure originality claims.

The Emergence of 16mm: Kodak's Strategy
Cinema spread rapidly all over the world but there were limits to this. The developed 35mm intermittent mechanism projector was scarcely portable (although obviously it was more portable than was the Biograph's 70mm one). Thus, 35mm did not readily abet the spread of motion picture exhibition both outside of urban areas and outside of dedicated spaces (cinemas) within urban areas. This was one problem. Secondly, 35mm also required cameras (and, of course, projectors) somewhat too large to be sold to the public, inhibiting the growth of amateur cinematography. The cameras were, compared with what was to emerge in the studios in the sound period, still portable but nevertheless at least three to four times the size of the ubiquitous Box Brownie with which Kodak had created a vast amateur market in still photography. Thus, virtually unnoticed behind the fantastic spread of cinema all over the world, 35mm nevertheless meant that non-theatrical exhibition was, however marginally, more limited than it might have been while an amateur market could not develop for cinematography at all easily.

Attempts to overcome these difficulties were made almost from the first, the idea of a substandard stock producing a number of what might be considered prototypes, the earliest being a slit 35mm film, i.e. 17.5 mm, introduced in London in 1898 by the British Lumière pioneer, Birt Acres. Pathé introduced 28mm in 1912 specifically to improve projector portability. This was accepted as the usual format for non-theatrical exhibition when the SMPE gave a measure of professional acknowledgment to it by establishing a (slightly different) US standard for 28mm stocks in 1918.[9]

The search for a non-theatrical projection standard could proceed without researchers worrying about another major problem – safety. The 35mm gauge was nitrocellulose-based and highly volatile. While narrower nitrate-based gauges, such as 28mm, would do as well (or as badly) from the fire hazard point of view as 35mm, there was a clear understanding that, for amateurs, nitrate was simply too dangerous. However, non-flammable or less-inflammable safety films were available before World War I, the earliest patent for such material being granted in 1904. Kodak 'were prepared to give up manufacture of nitrate and go entirely to acetate film' as early as 1909.[10] Three years later Edison Inc. marketed a 22mm safety stock for 'home, schools, YMCA, clubs, etc.' as being specifically 'APPROVED BY FIRE AUTHORITIES'.[11]

Despite this, nitrate stock was not finally to disappear from the industry until the early 50s, no less than half a century or so after the first patent for the safe alternative. This can be seen as a further elegant, or perhaps extreme, example of industrial conservatism; in effect, the power of suppressive forces inhibiting the introduction of new techniques and materials. I would here discount the claims made for the sparkling quality of the nitrate image as against the comparative 'muddiness' of safety. Even if true, the public were (and are) not so addicted to image quality as to render safety unmarketable. It seems to me reasonable to suggest that the industry basically clung to an extremely dangerous substance long after an alternative was available as much as a protection against competition as an earnest of its commitment to top-quality images. After all, only professionals could handle real films; only professionals could be, quite literally, licensed as projectionists and cinema managers, creating thereby at the most potentially dispersed end of the industry, exhibition, a coherent, identifiable and controllable element. The business protection that this provided was worth the odd projection booth conflagration.

The attempt to create a non-theatrical projection standard, whether on nitrate or safety, was soon abandoned in the United States. In 1918 the 28mm Pathéscope was being marketed by the Victor Animatograph Company of Iowa as 'Safety Cinema'; two years later, as a last hope, it was 'Home Cinema'. In this way, in the period up to 1920, 'substandard' gauges were abandoned for exhibition purposes and were increasingly used in the attempt to create an amateur market. In the US, the research and development of narrower stocks came to be seen as essential for amateur movie-making rather than for portable professional exhibition. This meant that such gauges were increasingly also limited to safety stock as well. The amateur Movette system of 1917 is a good example of where these tendencies were leading. It used a double-sprocketed 17.5mm nitrate negative but a safety positive.[12] But the amateur market proved to be no easier to establish than the non-theatrical exhibition market. It quickly became clear that these efforts to sell amateur movie-making were not producing the massive level of consumption that still photography had. There was no real supervening necessity for amateur movie-making.

Workers in the Kodak Research Laboratory continued to experiment 'from time to time' on 'substandard' cine-stocks nevertheless. The first pre-World War I phase of experimental work demonstrated that safety reversal film, which removed the need for an expensive additional positive print, would work. Reversal film is developed twice, producing first a negative and then a positive on the same base. Reversal safety film can be thought of as part of the competencies, the ground of science, available to the researchers. At the same time parallel experiments in image size were again determined by culture. A quarter, a sixth and an eighth of the 35mm frame size were tried and it was determined that a 10mm × 7.5mm frame – a quarter of 35mm – was the minimum viable and, consequently, a stock base 16mm wide ($^1/_2$" plus sprocket holes) was produced on reversal safety stock. This had the added safety and commercial advantage of creating a product which could not be derived directly from 35mm, as 17.5mm had been. (This work also demonstrated that any frame smaller than $^1/_6$th of the 35mm standard would not yield an acceptable image quality – until emulsion manufacture improved sufficiently to allow for a split 16mm stock, 8mm, by 1928. This was on the market four years later, in time to cushion Bell & Howell's Depression-hit 16mm sales revenues.[13])

The attitude within Kodak was somewhat confused, a reflection of the weak nature of the supervening social necessity. The lab workers regarded the faltering amateur market as a legitimate area for research, but George Eastman himself 'remained reluctant to enter a field of manufacture in which so many other firms had been unsuccessful'.[14] It is to his credit as an executive that he nevertheless authorised a development programme in 1916, on the basis of unofficial (as it were) work already done on reversal safety film, so that the company would have a product available just in case a rival did manage to create a market.

In Europe, Pathé maintained an active interest in substandard gauges as the key to non-theatrical exhibition even after 28mm had failed to make any real headway. In 1922 it decided to try something new, neither non-theatrical exhibition nor home movie-making. The firm introduced a Pathé Baby projector with a view to recycling its considerable 35mm film library directly to the public in the form of retail sales. Pathé Baby used a reversal safety film 9.5mm wide with a single perforation hole placed between the frames. This proved to be moderately popular with the French public so the company, the following year, followed up the projector with a camera.[15] The French could now buy films they had liked or missed in the cinema and expand their libraries with films shot by themselves. The market success then worked as the focus for the supervening social necessity; it made home movies a commercial and social reality.

This then forced others to innovate as well. The contingency Eastman Kodak had been concerned about for a decade appeared to be coming into play but they were ready to reply with 16mm. (Since the 9.5mm standard had a central sprocket between the frames, as opposed to sprockets on both sides of the frame in 16mm, the actual image sizes were less different than might be at first supposed.) Immediately, both Victor Animatograph and Bell & Howell introduced cameras and projectors for 16mm Ciné-Kodak. The SMPE moved very quickly to establish a 16mm standard in 1924. An Amateur Cinema League was founded in 1926 and its magazine, *Amateur Movie Makers,* appeared that December.[16] Amateur cinematography thus became an 'invention'.

As an example of far-sighted corporate strategy, Eastman's approach to the problems posed to the company by amateur cinematography cannot be faulted. A judicious, albeit comparatively low-key, research and development activity over a decade allowed the company instantly to respond to a potential pre-emptive challenge from a major competitor. The result was the establishment of a viable business and a fascinating area of film activity which has only recently began to receive appropriate scholarly attention.[17] But, because 16mm was labelled so firmly 'amateur', whole professional applications were left unexplored, and it is that failure which here concerns us.

That failure can be represented on the model at the top of page 63.

In effect, the weak market for amateur cinematography and strong objections to amateurism condemned 16mm to a sort of limbo until the social necessities created by World War II and post-war television transformed the situation.

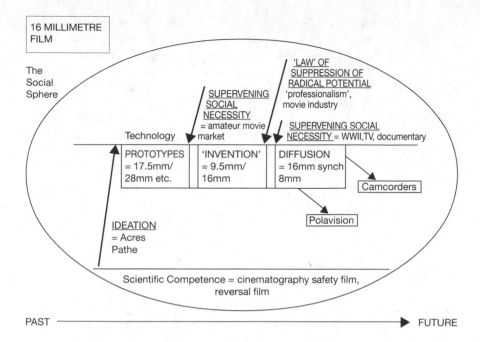

It will be objected that 16mm was unsuitable for projection in the vast cinemas that had become the norm and also that, after 1930, the gauge had the additional disadvantage that it could not accommodate sound; but such objections misunderstand the point. The question is: were these inadequacies the product of technology or attitude? If they were the latter, then we are dealing with the virtual suppression of a technology. Thus far I have shown that it was attitude and not technology which determined 35mm as the standard in the 1890s and that failed to exploit narrower gauges, including (after 1916) 16mm, until the mid-20s. By looking at the behaviour in the 1930s of those professionals who eventually came to use 16mm, that is news and documentary film-makers, I want to show how, once again, it was attitude and not technology which caused the research and development, necessary both to overcome the stock's initial limitations and to convert it from amateur to professional use, to be neglected.

Avoiding the Amateur (1): The Newsreels

As I have already suggested, it is easy to see why Hollywood ignored all developments in substandard stocks. The industry was so successful it did not even need to take note of 28mm or 22mm or any other gauge to create a niche non-theatrical market and it certainly did not want any dilution of the production norms which the barrier of the 35mm nitrate standard sustained and ensured. Home movies were thus quite distinct, not least exactly because they did not use 35mm.

Anyway, there was in effect only one area where the film industry might have reaped some advantage in the long term from the use of 16mm: newsreels. There were many reasons why this did not happen. In the first place, the technological limitations of 35mm as a newsgathering gauge were not so apparent as they were to become in the sound era. The earliest professional studio hand-cranked cameras, although unergonomic boxes designed for tripod operation, were of reasonable size and weight, easily usable even in remote and/or constricted exterior locations.

In the earliest years, newsreel items, actualities (*actualités*) or topicals, were sold by producers to exhibitors like any other sort of film. This meant that, although they were quite clearly situated as a filmic version of news, they needed shelf-life of greater duration than their announced topicality would imply. The solution, before the establishment of specialised theatres in the second decade of cinema, was

> to feature events of lasting interest. Major ceremonies of state, celebrated annual events and big sporting occasions were the favoured subjects since these kept their sale value. Otherwise stories of an on-going nature, such as a war or the suffragette issue, could be filmed and the same film exploited over a period of time.[18]

Luke McKernan suggests that this situation changed somewhat with the establishment of dedicated theatres (cinemas) which could profitably show reels for just a few days. This was done first with the *actualités* pioneered in France by Pathé and Gaumont; but, although the material produced by the emergent specialised newsreel companies (or newsreel divisions of more general production companies) could now be more topical, this did not happen to any great extent.[19] Despite the norm of two editions a week being rapidly established, twice-weekly publication did not mean that the essential concept of the useless-if-delayed 'perishability' of printed news was seriously transferred to the new medium. The production cycle was usually too slow for spot news and anyway the strange compromise with topicality that had characterised the first actuality shorts had not prevented them becoming popular with the public. Why push for ever quicker turn-round times? Instead, the newsreel companies came to compete by way of stunts and gimmicks rather than with hard-news scoops.

All this was despite the term '*news*reel' (introduced in the US in 1917) and the fact the names of the established reels in the decade prior to that, *Gazette, Graphic, Chronicle* and so on, were obviously copied from the press. The occasional rapid turn-round, for example, on the Grand National, where the footage was shown the same day or even, in McKernan's phrase, 'a freakishly early attempt' to create a daily reel in London in 1906, are therefore the exceptions that prove the rule. Cinema grew up with a different vision of what constituted the news. Essentially, the curious version of topicality established in the founding moments was never abandoned in favour of a more responsive news agenda. This meant that the nearest the early newsreel men came to breaking news was, from World War I on, to add to their schedules '"sudden events" [which had prolonged aftermaths] like the Japanese earthquake' to '"impending events" whose occurrence might be predicted from existing situations, such as the burning of Smyrna during the 1922 war between the Greeks and the Turks; and "scheduled events" such as ball-games, coronations and inaugurations'.[20] From the very beginning, then, newsreels were doomed to be the 'six catastrophes concluded with a fashion show' which Oscar Levant was to satirise in the 1960s.[21] (In this avoidance of hard news, of course, they were like our contemporary tabloids; but, in the early years of the cinema newsreels, contemporary popular newspapers were still slightly more serious. The sort of entertaining quasi-journalism that now fills our tabloids – and always filled the newsreels – was then to be found more in publications that eschewed 'news' in general.)

This failure to establish a real news agenda, determined by the terms of film distribution in the first years of the century, was compounded by (or, perhaps, created by) the personnel involved in newsreel production. The earliest newsreel producers tended to be exactly the same sort of showmen who were to found the great fiction-producing studios, and, although companies like Pathé and Gaumont were joined by press interests such as Hearst in America and Harmsworth in Britain, the ownership of the reels in general remained more show business than news business. This distance from journalism was reflected as much in the newsreels' editors as it was in their owners, although there is some dispute about this. George Woods-Taylor, the first news editor of the UK reel *Topical Budget*, was a Fleet Street photographer but was rare in rising to an editorial position. Most who came from photojournalism mainly operated in the newsreels as cinematographers and climbed no higher.[22] The managers were usually from a different world. For instance, at *Movietone* the editor-in-chief was Sir Malcolm Campbell, the racing driver, and the executive producer was Gerald Sanger whose connection with journalism was that he had been a private secretary to one of the Harmsworths. Conversely, it is easy to find production executives and editorial directors with long film-industry experience.[23]

In the final analysis, the extent to which journalists were or were not involved in newsreel production does not matter. As has been very well documented, the reels almost totally failed to cover any of the major stories of the 30s (except the wars) and thereby lost all credibility with the public.[24] Even if journalists were involved editorially, they might as well not have been.

Obviously, given that covering the dictators, the Depression and spot news was not what the newsreels were about, there was not much impetus coming from the editorial side to produce cameras that would allow for a more investigative and thorough approach to be taken. And all this remained true even after the coming of sound. The old intertitles simply gave way to voice-over commentary plus music and a few effects, so that most shooting could, to all intents and purposes, remain silent, even where (as at *Movietone*) much was made of synch sound. At the outset, sound meant a rig that could weigh up to 1,400lbs. By the mid-30s it was down to 150lbs.[25] Either way, only the most formal situations could be filmed in synch. The obvious limitations of sound were dealt with by simply ignoring the challenge. Location sound, except for the stultifyingly deferential interviews with authorities of all kinds that became a feature of the reels in the later 30s, remained exceptional.

Wars could be covered as they had been between 1914–18 with old-style silent cameras; but, equally unadventurously, even handholding these was not explored. As the publicity photographs tend to reveal, camera operators always used tripods. After all, these approaches had carried cinematography into every corner of the world and covered World War I. Neither the coming of sound nor the worsening international situation nor the growing strength of radio news required a rethink. There was never any question of the news-reels offering a serious view of the world and a window on what was happening in it. This failure of the newsreel industry to establish an effective research and development programme for 16mm was entirely reasonable by main-stream film-making logic. The audience came, millions upon millions a week, so why worry? In short, the newsreels had less than no supervening necessity to switch gauges, however much newsgathering might have been improved by such a move.

Avoiding the Amateur (2): The Documentary Movement
The parallel avoidance of alternatives to 35mm by the documentarists who emerged in the 1930s is more difficult to explain.

Although the UK Documentary Movement was officially funded and dedicated to a programme of public education, this did not prevent it from positioning itself both by rhetoric and in practice as being an alternative to the mainstream film industry. Not only did it produce films very different from the industry but it also came to hypothesise a different relationship with its audience and to push for alternative distribution and exhibition systems. It can be argued that this was forced upon the documentarists when their films failed to established a firm place in the cinema programmes of the day because they were largely unpopular with audiences and suspect because of official sponsorship.[26] But whatever the reason, there is no question that there was a push for alternative systems of exhibition outside the theatres. John Grierson, the leader of the British Documentary Movement, wrote in 1935: 'As I see it, the future of the cinema may not be in the cinema at all.'[27]

Curiously, however, this vision was never translated into a programme of technological innovation. Certainly not much consideration was given to how non-theatrical exhibition could be encouraged by the use of 16mm. As a result, by 1939 for instance, only 1,700 British schools had 16mm projectors and of these only 400 were equipped for sound.[28] Even less consideration was given to the impact 16mm might have on documentary film production.

I believe that this failure of vision can be directly attributed to the fact that, although it had not matched the ubiquitousness of the Box Brownie, 16mm had nevertheless become over the previous decade so firmly established as an amateur stock that using it would have simply diminished the stature of the documentarists as 'professionals'. It would have made them amateurs – automatically as it were. This danger was sufficient to outweigh any needs they might have had for equipment more suitable than the 35mm studio gear they were forced to use in carrying out their stated first principle of 'getting around ... observing and selecting from life itself'.[29]

Not that there was anything wrong with amateurs as Basil Wright, a leading Documentary Movement director, acknowledged when, in 1938 for *Amateur Ciné World*, he suggested they were 'a potential force for social and civic values'.[30] However, when Grierson, that same year, advised them to use 16mm for helping worthy causes make promotional films on the cheap, he exactly thereby distinguished himself from them. They might have potential in 16mm; he had achievements in 35mm. The ACT, the British film technicians' union, saw his recommendation as threatening the unemployed technician in the depressed industrial movie sector; such people were, apparently, prepared to shoot on 16mm but only if that were the only available job.[31]

It must not be thought, though, that these professional film-makers were unaware of the potential of 16mm for the documentary. Wright, for instance, seemed to be envious of the amateurs: 'they have ... the possibilities of technique denied to workers on standard film, who are bound by bulky apparatus and who are to some extent denied the intimacies which go with a light and easily worked hand-camera.'[32] Yet the advantages the smaller gauge would yield were not sufficient to compensate for the loss of status. This was not merely a question of snobbery. As Patricia Zimmermann points out, over the previous century and more, professionalism in all walks of life had become an expression of the public sphere; amateurism could be defined conversely as being an expression of the private sphere.[33] Therefore Grierson had no option but to ignore 16mm since, as a technology of the private sphere, it was, as it were, inconceivable that it could be of value for his public-sphere, public-education project.[33] Professional documentarists ignored 16mm.

Avoiding the Amateur (3): The Radicals and the Ethnographers

There was more of a debate about alternative production methods outside of the Documentary Movement in the world of left-independent film-makers, but even here there seemed to be little structural understanding of the role of film technology as such. The arguments turned on the nature of Hollywood as the prime player in the consciousness industry and the need to produce socialist films by way of a response. Thus, although 16mm, as an uncensored – as it was at the time in the UK – non-nitrate gauge, was exploited by some groups for exhibition purposes, the broader theoretical and ideological possibilities were not widely discussed. For instance, the left knew that the police were beginning to use 16mm for surveillance[34] but this sort of phenomenon did not seem to provoke any deeper understanding. The technologies were considered neutral.

This was not quite true of everybody. Some did see 16mm as 'the avenue to progress': 'the 16mm camera in the right hands is no toy'; 'Sub-standard is the only way out.'[35] As early as 1931, German radicals were calling attention to 16mm.[36] Agitprop films began to appear in that gauge and in 9.5mm, but the reason was usually expediency, normally cost considerations. But, in special local circumstances, film-makers could be forced to take advantage of the smaller size for other reasons. For instance, in Japan 16mm was used because state repression rendered all such film-making illegal. The smaller equipment facilitated secret shooting.[37] In Britain, by Bert Hogenkamp's count, the largest single group of titles in the independents' archive – 53 per cent of the 93 films made during the 30s by agitprop groups – were silent 16mm productions. A further 7 per cent were 16mm sound films.[38] Nevertheless, the common view was that there was an 'amazing lack of good sub-calibre film work'.[39] Film-makers had to be forced to use 16mm, and, wherever it could be avoided, it was. In the US, for instance, the radicals continued with silent 35mm not least because the coming of sound had made the old studio cameras obsolete and cheap and the occasional theatrical screening was facilitated by using the wider gauge.[40] The point is that 16mm of itself never became a rallying point for alternative film production in the 30s.

Lacking the luxury of official sponsorship, many radical film-makers were forced to use 16mm only to run the risk of being branded as amateurs. And branded as amateurs they were. Film critic Rudolph Messel was one of the first to appreciate that 16mm made film-making possible and, in 1933, started the Socialist Films Council after locating eight 16mm projectors. Typically, Paul Rotha, although the mainstream Documentary Movement's most left-wing voice, dismissed the first efforts of the Council, *The Road to Hell* and *What the Newsreels Do Not Show*, as '*amateur* and immature' (emphasis added).[41]

The independents had no reply to this, not least because they too made a straightforward distinction between amateur and professional without any discussion of the ideological implications of so doing. There was a constant appeal to the court of professionalism. Ralph Bond, a leading light of the workers' film movement, was insisting that 'adequate care, thought and attention must be given to all amateur production ... hastily conceived and shoddily executed work will only bring discredit'.[42] The remedy to amateurism lay in study – for instance of Pudovkin's *Film Technique* and the work of Fritz Lang.[43] Needless to say, the notion that these aesthetic 'standards', however apparently revolutionary some of them might be, might inhibit free expression because they were derived from professional productions was not on the agenda.[44]

The only group of film-makers who brought any degree of deeper understanding to the possibilities of 16mm technology in the 30s were the ethnographers. Only they seemed to have any sense that there might be intrinsic advantages in using substandard. For instance, in the series on *Character Formation in Different Cultures*, Margaret Mead and Gregory Bateson determined that actions such as bathing babies could be better observed if the film was shot on 16mm. Cost obviously had something to do with this but for Mead and Bateson, as well as for other pioneers such as Norman Tindale filming Australian aboriginals and Franz Boas working with Native Americans in Canada, there was also, not surprisingly, a sensitivity to the impact of filming on the processes of observation which was lacking in less sophisticated and scientific film-makers. Margaret Mead explained that she and Bateson had abandoned 35mm (and the usual accompaniment of a professional cinematographer) because she needed to record 'types of non-verbal behaviour for which there existed neither vocabulary nor conceptualized methods of observation'.[45] She needed not to get in the way and she needed to film.

This is without prejudice as to how successful or not she might have been in such ambitions; it is simply to point out that anthropologists were aware, as were almost no others, that 16mm might have advantages when it came to using the camera to gather scientific (or documentary) evidence. The shift to 16mm was accompanied by the removal of the professional cameramen who had usually accompanied that minority of anthropological expeditions which had used film at all. The result was, as it were, the de-professionalisation of the filmed ethnography – at least from the point of view of other professional film-makers. The move to 16mm, for all that it might have enhanced film as a ethnographic tool from the anthropologists' point of view, did nothing for their status as professional film-makers. Put another way, using substandard marks a shift from (to use the terms of David MacDougall) 'finished film' (i.e. edited 35mm works obeying, more or less, 'standard' structural norms) to 'record footage' (i.e. unedited or minimally edited 16mm field notes).[46] Most of the ethnographers who used the medium did not make the move and films were still being shot on 35mm well into the 50s.[47]

I am suggesting there is an interplay here between the attitudes of news-reel producers and documentarists which had substandard firmly fixed as an amateur gauge and which resulted in a collective failure to develop 16mm as a viable professional medium. The use of 16mm by non-amateur (as it were) agitprop film-makers and ethnographers did not help the gauge's cause.

However, demonstrating that a negative attitude (or lack of supervening need) existed still leaves the question of whether or not 16mm *could* have been developed in the 30s to meet professional expectations. Certainly it was 'commonly supposed' that the 'amazing lack of good sub-calibre film work' was not just because of the failings of those who used the gauge but was also intrinsic to it.[48] There is, though, no reason to believe this was the case. After all, 16mm required no real breakthroughs to become established during and after World War II. Its technical deficiencies in the 30s were already negligible in the sense that when the circumstances arose requiring they be fixed, they were fixed – fast.

Suppressing 16mm's Potential
Cameras designed for 16mm were clockwork driven but 35mm cameras all had electric motors. This was not a problem since the smaller cameras could be given electric motors without difficulty. Similarly, 16mm cameras lacked a full range of prime lenses but, again, professional demand could easily have caused those lenses to be ground. The same applies to other camera accessories such as filters. More significantly, emulsions were undergoing steady improvement even for amateurs to the point where, by 1932, as we have seen, it was possible to produce a reasonable (if small) projected image from a frame one-sixteenth the area of 35mm – 8mm. Such responsiveness obviously also improved the quality of 16mm. Finally, even the serious difficulties of

sound could have been tackled. How this could have been accomplished impacts not only on the development of 16mm but also on Hollywood studio practice as well. The technology of seeing 16mm now requires a slight detour into sound recording techniques.

For much the same underlying economic reasons as had produced the dominance of 35mm and the hegemony of Technicolor, the Hollywood industry similarly opted for cumbersome and expensive sound systems. It ignored developments which would have allowed for the miniaturisation of equipment with consequent reductions in cost. The essence of this barriers-to-entry strategy can be seen in the failure of the industry seriously to explore the possibilities of tape sound systems, a history which has been recovered by William Lafferty.[49]

From the first, movies and sound had gone hand-in-hand. Although live music in the cinema rapidly became the industry norm, there were also lecturers explaining the film and even actors reading a script behind the screen as well. At the same time, from the very start of the cinema, there were attempts to link sound and picture mechanically. As we have seen in Chapter One, Muybridge approached Edison with this possibility for his Zoopraxiscope. Although this was not pursued, William Dickson had linked his boss's phonograph to the Kinetoscope and, repeatedly, this sort of approach was to be explored.

Carl Laemmle tried to get Paramount into the synchronised disk business in 1907. (Disks were developed between 1876-8 by Emile Berliner.)[50] In 1908 forty-five cinemas were screening sound films in the US.[51] The 'fad' passed but this setback in completely mechanising theatrical entertainment at least preserved the musicians' jobs. Considered from this angle, the failure to introduce mechanical sound was an element constraining the cinema's radical potential to disrupt the theatre industry. Nevertheless, more attempts were made. In 1913 Edison, with a system he called the Kinetophone, and Gaumont with *films parlants*, both tried to introduce disk systems. A decade or so later what was to be the last try to diffuse synchronised projectors and gramophones was made. *Don Juan*, a film with synchronised music disks was premiered by Warners in August, 1926. Warners called the method, which had been developed by AT&T's subsidiary Western Electric, the Vitaphone. *The Jazz Singer* followed in October 1927.[52]

Warners was not an industry leader, a significant factor contributing to its interest in sound, and an equally significant reason why its preferred system was not to prevail. In fact, it was struggling to break into the top rank of studios. With the help of a credit line provided by bankers Goldman Sachs, Warners had embarked on a cinema acquisition programme and general expansion. To promote its films, the company bought a radio station which brought it into contact with Western Electric and the possibility of sound films.[53]

The optical sound recording system that Hollywood adopted in 1927 instead of Vitaphone has its origins in a continuous stream of devices designed to make sound visible in some way, largely as aids in the education of the deaf. Alexander Graham Bell, given his background in this field, was

70

one of the most significant of early researchers. Prior to 1880, he began conducting experiments in transmitting speech using a beam of light as a carrier wave.[55] The crucial concept in applying this idea to film was that the sound thus made visible and the photographic image could be combined on the same strip of celluloid for projection, unlike rival disk systems where projector and gramophone were, obviously, separate. The idea of combining an optical soundtrack with the image was patented in 1907 by Eugene Lauste, one of the original team who had worked on the Kinetoscope. He is believed to have made the first combined soundtrack by 1910, using a system of rocking mirrors and a light bulb.[55]

Electronic photographic sound recording, with amplifying valves (tubes), was a readily available technological option after World War I; and Lee de Forest, a pioneer of such devices, spent the 20s applying their use to the problem of sound film. In his system (and all like it), sound waves are translated (transduced) into an electrical wave, via a microphone (microphones were introduced in 1878). The wave produced by the mike is then used to vary the intensity of a current powering a light bulb which, in consequence, flickers, these variations being exposed on film. The result is a visible recorded analogue of the original wave. De Forest, and his sometime partner Theodore Case, were not alone in the research to make such a system in the metal. Tonbild Syndicat-Tobis in Germany and Tonfilm in Denmark were exploiting the same technology, as were others in Europe, with the inevitable resultant patent battles.[56]

In America, Case contributed his refinement of de Forest's tube to Fox Studios and the result was the Movietone system. Fox, like Warners, was another of the smaller studios and its exploitation of sound reinforced Warner's comparative success. The five major firms, Paramount-Famous Players-Lasky, Metro-Goldwyn-Mayer, United Artists, Universal and First National, had been sceptical about sound. Some, like Paramount, had a history of failed experiments; but now the success of Warner's vaudeville shorts and Fox's *Movietone News* forced movement.

The Big Five, avoiding Warners' Vitaphone and the Case/Fox Movietone, bought an alternative optical contrivance, Westrex, from Western Electric. They could do this because de Forest had patent arrangements with AT&T. AT&T's philosophy at the Bell Labs was to exploit all possibilities simultaneously. There was no difficulty in marketing a disk system (Vitaphone) and an optical system (Westrex) at the same time. De Forest had a good patent position against Case, and therefore against Fox and Movietone; and Bell anyway had the best loudspeakers, whatever recording technology was chosen. More worrying was the fact that General Electric, Westinghouse and RCA were also working in the area of optical sound.

There was to be no patent battle, though. The end of the matter was that all these players negotiated among themselves cross-patent agreements to produce two effective (and compatible in the projector) sound-on-film systems. One was created by GE and Westinghouse and marketed by RCA as the Photophone; the other was based on the Western Electric/Bell system and was exploited by a wholly-owned subsidiary of AT&T, the

Electrical Research Products Inc. (ERPI). ERPI rapidly became the dominant player in Hollywood.[57] The Westrex system was the most technologically accomplished not least because, in this series of deals, it had combined the best elements from Bell, General Electric and Movietone. In part as a consequence of this, it was also the most expensive system available. Converting the studios to sound cost between $23,000,000 and $50,000,000.[58] The end result was that Westrex optical sound was a near monopoly controlled by AT&T, through ERPI, via its Western Electric subsidiary.[59] ERPI was in no doubt as to what this meant by the mid-30s. One of its executives could tell the parent AT&T board that: 'It is true today, as it has been for three or four years, that the Telephone Company can control the motion picture industry'.[60]

Because of the Big Five's decision in its favour, Western Electric was able to take over the Fox optical system and to close down Warner's Vitaphone in the early 30s. AT&T was untroubled by the existence of one last rival, RCA, because it protected them against the government using its anti-monopoly legislation. The Big Five had no trouble with the situation because the RCA system was equally expensive. The more expensive and complicated the industry standard (cf. Technicolor), the less chance of them being again caught napping by a Warners. Optical sound thus becomes a barrier to entry, deliberately erected.

This well-known series of developments also impacted on 16mm. The same principles could be applied to create soundtracks for the narrower gauge and 16mm prints with optical tracks were soon introduced. The Bell & Howell Filmosound, introduced in 1932, became the most popular optical 16mm sound projector in the world.[61] But there was a real question mark over the possibility of *shooting* 16mm sound. In 1933 Eric Knight, writing in *Cinema Quarterly*, reported in some dudgeon that in 1931 the SMPE had declared publicly that 16mm sound-on-film was impossible'. He offered the most strenuous rebuttal possible to this: 'Recently I made a film with the "impossible" [sound] camera created by RCA-Victor.'[62]

Although he made extravagant claims for the quality of the sound, he admitted that the camera, which recorded in a single system onto the same piece of celluloid as held the image, was not very flexible. Single system combined optical sound (comopt) was good for exhibition but caused problems in post-production because the sound relating to any one frame is necessarily displaced. This means that editing synch comopt is nearly impossible, unless the sound is re-recorded onto separate stock. Hence the creation of a separate optical sound camera which recorded the track on a second strip of 35mm celluloid – a double system which permits fully flexible editing. The image and sound were brought together, using the synch marks created by the clapper board. Later they could be combined for final prints.

All of this could have been duplicated in 16mm, but obviously it would be far too elaborate as long as the industry insisted that it was a non-professional gauge. Knight saw that: 'Possibly the construction of such cameras must be worked out by ingenious amateurs who will guide the mass-production men.'[63] It was to be another twenty-five years before this dream of a flexible separate sound and vision double system was to be produced in 16mm. When it happened it was to use the sound technology that Hollywood had ignored – magnetic tape.

Magnetic recording had been introduced with a machine, developed by Valdemar Poulsen by 1898, which used wire as the recording medium. The device had never been widely diffused. In part, this can be attributed to the fact that it recorded at high speed, ten feet per second to capture a mere 2,000 cycles, but there is also some evidence that, in the United States at least, AT&T intervened actively to disrupt and frustrate the affairs of the Poulsen company. One purpose suggested for the machine by Poulsen was to make the recording of telephone conversations possible. This made the telephone company fearful for the security of the phone-call and the legal implications of telephony becoming a communication system of record. Therefore, during World War I, AT&T played no little part in killing these first magnetic recording devices.[64] Nevertheless, Lee de Forest himself attempted to run an early wire recorder in synch with a projector in 1913. The first patent for such a system dates from 1915. In the 20s Max Krohle and Kurt Stille substituted metal drums or steel disks for the wire. Stille even produced a perforated steel strip for film-recording purposes.[65] In 1928 Dr Sydney Baruch repeated de Forest's demonstration publicly and promised the film industry an inexpensive alternative to both disk and optical systems. He did not deliver.

The most sustained attempt to put magnetic recording in synch with film took place in Britain where a German émigré film producer, Ludwig Blattner, the founder of Elstree Studios, endeavoured to exploit Stille's steel tape system. First demonstrated in 1929, it was effective and delivered a sound cleaner than that produced by the optical Tobis system, at least for speech. The BBC used the device to rebroadcast programming in its Empire Service. Blattner failed to establish the technology and, when he went bankrupt in 1933, Marconi took up the licence. They then worked with the BBC to refine the machines which were used by the Corporation throughout the 30s.[66]

Modern audiotape, using metallic particles embedded onto a flexible base rather than a wholly metal medium like steel tape, was developed in Germany in this same period by Fritz Plfeumer. By 1934 BASF were manufacturing tape on a cellulose acetate base, just like film except for the fact that, because of the coating, it was, of course, opaque. The tape was 5cm wide and could be several hundred metres long. By 1937 AEG was using BASF tape in its Magnetophon recorder and in 1938 the German State Broadcasting authority, the RRG, adopted the machine.[67] The Nazi leaders had all their wartime speeches preserved using this device. Despite the close ties maintained by many British and American high-tech firms with their German subsidiaries, offshoots, and partners throughout the Nazi era,[68] the Magnetophon remained uniquely German. Like the Marconi-Stille steel tape device, its use was limited to radio.

Magnetic recording was therefore a demonstrated alternative to both disk and optical sound. It was certainly the case that the quality of all these devices was somewhat suspect, but in 1939 an RRG engineer, Walter Weber, seeking to reduce the Magnetophon's 'noise', added a circuit that accidentally produced a full high-fidelity recording. Weber used a technique first described in America in 1918. The point here is that it took nothing more than serious attention from a major user to achieve this result. Despite some specialised use, radio was committed to live transmission and therefore had little interest in going beyond the recording technologies it already had to hand. But it could have been such a user and achieved the hi-fi break through earlier. The film industry is in like case.

There is the difficulty that the BASF tape was conceived of by Plfeumer even as the studios were converting to optical sound. His innovation, although a variant on the steel strips of Stille and the celluloid of film, was nevertheless extremely original and, I acknowledge, is not prefigured in the way Weber's advance was. Given the speed with which optical was introduced in 1929,[69] it is possible that tape was simply too late. But conversely: 'Technologically ... the period from 1926 to the middle of the 1930s was chaotic';[70] and the studios were in the grip of a virtual monopoly situation with optical sound. On balance, although exhibition was tied to optical, there is certainly no reason why tape should have not made its way into the production process at other points, as, indeed, it was eventually to do thirty years later. Yet it was ignored by the industry.

After the war, Magnetophon patents were appropriated by the US Alien Property Custodian and commercially exploited first by Ampex who introduced a pioneering studio audiotape deck to the US radio industry in 1947. The British also appropriated the patents and, in the UK, the Ampex role was played by EMI. The engineer who facilitated the American development, Jack Mullin, was well aware of film as a potential market as well, not least because he owned a third share in a small production company. He demonstrated a tape deck at MGM in October 1946;[71] but Hollywood was still uninterested, at least for production. Nevertheless, by 1947 specialised companies were making sprocketed tape (mag sound stock) in 16mm and 35mm formats. Putting a magnetic stripe down one side of the image, in the place where the optical track fits, was done soon after.[72] (The idea of the mag stripe had been patented twenty years earlier, in 1927, by Joseph O'Neill.[73]) It was used for widescreen releases. Mag stripe was also available for specialised 16mm distribution purposes from the early 50s; for instance, in the preparation of multiple-language prints.

As tape became the norm in radio stations, in the record industry, in the home, then in television stations as videotape, and even for specialised film distribution purposes, Hollywood remained committed to the cumbersome optical sound cameras it had been using for the last thirty and more years. Finally, by the early 60s even Hollywood was ready for a magnetic recorder on a sound stage and optical slowly disappeared except for the making of release prints.

Supervening Necessity: Stage 1 – World War II
The existence of a more or less viable magnetic recording system, which a measure of sustained R&D would likely have perfected – as it was to do

after the war – is the final element in my argument that it was attitude not technology which held 16mm back professionally in the 30s. The point was that nobody using 35mm *needed* 16mm. Indeed, for most users of the professional gauge, there were good and cogent reasons to avoid 16mm. But World War II started to change this. In fact, nothing less than 'the militarization of all amateur-film equipment' took place.[74] New notions of film as an educational and morale-boosting tool for the citizens' armies of the democracies required a degree of portability previously eschewed by the film industry. The forces needed to be able to show films everywhere for propaganda/education and entertainment purposes. The critical decision was made to distribute films of all kinds to the American armed forces in 16mm format.[75] This constituted the earliest element of a supervening social necessity. It was the first strike against 16mm's amateur status, as, during World War II, the 35mm projector's bulk at last caught up with it. The result was that 16mm with optical sound became firmly established as an exhibition format. For much the same sort of reasons, others followed the American military lead. The British Ministry of Information, for example, also began a serious programme of 16mm distribution for civilian audiences.[76]

This breakthrough did not immediately transform the production situation. Combat could still be covered, now increasingly in a hand-held mode, by comparatively small 35mm silent (that is noisy) cameras, notably the clockwork-driven Bell & Howell 35mm Eyemos (introduced in 1925) and the superior electric-powered German Arriflex 35 (introduced in 1937). Nevertheless, improvements to 16mm production equipment were in train. 'The quality of lenses improved and parts [were] standardised and made interchangeable.'[77] In Britain, expansion of 16mm finally created a market for the first full-service film lab in that gauge, in 1942 at Denham.[78] In this way, 16mm was slowly (to use Robert Allen's phrase) 'professionalised' for telemetry and for the production of training films in World War II.

Supervening Necessity: Stage 2 – TV News
These various developments of 16mm as a gauge for prints, the potential of magnetic sound and improvements to the cameras meant that 16mm was ready to go professional. All that was needed was a further supervening social necessity.

The development of television news in America, which also occurred to a lesser and slower degree around the world, created a widespread need for cinematographic apparatus smaller and more mobile than that developed for the film studios. And the film equipment, as it was miniaturised, had to be less expensive than studio equivalents. TV stations, heavily committed to capital-intensive electronic studio complexes, were not likely to maximise investment in film at the same level as the film studios had. This did not mean, however, that TV could avoid professional film standards, just because Hollywood had, as it were, over-elaborated the equipment. TV was not necessarily, therefore, looking to work on film. Indeed, the early battle between New York and Los Angeles, between radio and the studios, to see who would dominate the medium had an element of technological rivalry in it exactly along these lines – electronics in New York versus film in Hollywood. But how far could New York avoid film? Drama (if not still made in Hollywood on 35mm) might well be totally transferable to the electronic studio. Game shows, variety, children's TV and current affairs debate could go the same way. But film was still needed, nationally and locally, to illustrate the news. Thus, if news were to be provided economically but still to a professional standard, it would have to be on a 16mm gauge readied for a new professional production role.

This need was generated by no mere whim on the part of the American networks and recently established television stations to do news. They had little option in the matter. The Federal Communications Commission, which had licensed the stations, had always been attached to localism as an element in its understanding of what constituted 'the public interest' in broadcasting. It now indicated that no better way of fulfilling the public interest regulatory requirement was available to these stations than the provision of local news broadcasts.[79] When these broadcasts proved to be among the most popular and profitable of all local originations, 16mm was at last assured of a future as a professional gauge. (In stressing the importance of the local element I do not intend to ignore the significance of the networks and their national news operations. They certainly made the running as early adopters of the emerging range of 16mm professional equipment. However, in this context, the creation of a full-scale market for 16mm required a combination of local and network newsfilm operations needing cameras and other equipment.)

This did not mean that the development of news as a presentational form in this newly diffused medium of television was without its own problems. The central issue, through the earliest period of experiments from 1935 on into the wartime test transmissions and the beginnings of the public system in the late 40s, was how to blend the radio news with the cinema newsreel. Radio news broadcasts were serious, immediate and, obviously, unillustrated. Newsreels were, as I have indicated, trivial and stale but, obviously, pictorial. How to put the two together in a coherent way was by no means obvious, not least because the newsreels themselves were still caught with an attitude to breaking stories conditioned by pre-World War I *actualité* producers.[80] No systematic attempt had been made to speed up the turn-round time of film or to develop special film equipment for newsgathering beyond what had emerged during World War II.

The nascent US television industry was committed by regulatory pressure and public demand to news production and by economic constraints to 16mm. Against this background, some designers were already thinking that 16mm might have a professional future and were adapting their 35mm cameras to the smaller gauge. Most significant among these were the German firm of Arnold and Richter. As I have said, they had introduced the Arriflex 35 just before World War II. Designed by August Arnold, this camera was unveiled at the Leipzig Fair in 1937 and had rapidly established itself as a classic.[81] It was the world's first mirror-reflex motion-picture camera. The eyepiece looked through the taking lens even while the film was being exposed, thus eliminating parallax problems (i.e. 'the difference between the composition of objects in the picture as seen through the viewfinder and through the camera lens').[82] The camera, even if it was unblimped (i.e. noisy, ergo 'silent' because only usable for non-synch shooting), was nevertheless also amazingly small. A picture of Arnold with the prototype shows it mounted only on a unipod. Other publicity shots of the 30s also show it hand-held. Richter accepted an Oscar for the camera in 1967.

There was no technical reason why this camera could not have been scaled down for 16mm in the pre-war period had there been any professional demand for such a device. Obviously a 16mm version of the Arri 35 would have been too expensive for amateurs and, as 16mm was still being thought of in amateur terms only, it was not built until after the war. Arnold then shrank his current 35, the II C, into a 16mm version, the 16 St. Professionals already knew and appreciated Arriflex quality. During the war Allied film crews were delighted to capture the enemies' Arris and put aside their extremely user-hostile 35mm Bell & Howells. Thus, the 16 St, after its introduction in the early 50s, quickly became ubiquitous. Within twenty years more than 20,000 had been sold, a considerable number considering the relative smallness of the potential market involved.[83]

Bell & Howell had no need of this down-sizing strategy since, paradoxically, the successful 35mm wartime camera, the Eyemo, had actually been derived from their first 16mm camera, the extremely rugged Filmo 70, initially introduced in 1923. In this sense Bell & Howell reverses the Arriflex story. Instead of not building a 16mm version of a 35mm camera until the post-war period, the American firm had built a 35mm version of a 16mm camera as soon as it had proved to be successful. The success of the Filmo did not alter 16mm's status; neither did the fact that the Eyemo was virtually identical make it amateur. On the contrary, the simple fact that it took 35mm film was enough to make it professional. The Filmo was still being marketed for home movies while its 35mm incarnation was hitting the beaches at Anzio. Production of the Filmo continued after the war and into the late 70s but, with 8mm playing the home movie role, the camera was now seen as a professional tool. Thus, despite a positively bizarre through-the-lens focusing system (unusable while shooting) and serious parallax problems, the Filmo had a production run of more than half a century from 1923 to 1979. It metamorphosed: the first 16mm movie camera for amateurs became a rugged camera for TV film news and other factual film-makers which in turn became (for example) the initial training camera used in the world's biggest film school[84] – exactly because the difficulties of operating it were considered a necessary part of 'professional' education.

The Arri St also had another direct competitor in the Paillard Bolex, a spring-driven camera which was widely prized by professionals and wealthy amateurs alike. It was a lot more user-friendly than the Filmo. The Bolex H16 was preferred for ethnographic work where electrical supply was impossible and batteries, as were needed by an St, could not be recharged. Bolex produced versions of the H16 with electric motors. Another firm, Beaulieu (or 'Bewley' as British camera operators seemed to insist on calling it), also produced a sophisticated electric-driven camera with innovations such as the first behind-the-lens light-metering system; but this RC16, introduced in 1964, was never seen as anything other than a somewhat exotic substitute for the St.[85] The Japanese never considered the 16mm professional potential market large enough to compete for and only one camera was offered by a Japanese manufacturer – the Cannon Scoopic. It enjoyed an even more limited success than the RC16. These cameras, despite being 16mm, were certainly pieces of professional equipment and as such were widely used for TV news and documentary productions of all kinds. But they were all silent (i.e. noisy).

The market created and served by the Arri, the Filmo and the Bolex did not however go unnoticed by those manufacturing 35mm sound (that is silent-running) cameras. These, too, could be scaled down for 16mm. Walter Bach pioneered this when he built a smaller copy of his typically square, silent-running (self-blimped), tripod-mounted 35mm studio camera. Bach's 16mm camera, the Auricon, used miniature valves (tubes) of the sort which had been developed for the military. Like Eric Knight's RCA-Victor twenty years earlier, it had a built-in optical sound system which allowed both sound and picture to be recorded on the same stock. Bach had reduced the camera to a reasonable size for most 16mm sound applications as they were understood in the early 50s – that is, TV news. This meant news pictures once again as steady as they had been in the 30s since only war coverage licensed hand-holding. The essentially unergonomic quality of Bach's design did not therefore matter much. The camera was made to be tripod mounted. In the technical literature, both texts and advertisements, the Auricon is shown mounted on a standard wooden tripod with large head. The operator is wearing headphones and twiddling with the camera's small external sound amplifier which he (inevitably) has on a shoulder strap.

At the end of 1955 Bach announced an interesting modification to this range – magnetic sound.[86] In May 1956, at the SMPTE convention, he more fully described the development, called the Filmagnetic, clearly indicating his intended market: 'Particularly for TV newsreel work, where ... soundtrack and picture are recorded on the same film at the same time, followed by fast film-processing and editing to exploit the "news" value, many difficulties are encountered in obtaining top-quality sound and picture ... '[87] These difficulties were essentially that local regional labs, while able to produce good-quality pictures, had far greater problems with optical tracks, 'particularly on a "rush" newsreel basis'.[88] Here then was an innovation apparently coming from what I have been positioning as a bastion of technological conservatism, Hollywood. Was the Los Angeles-based Bach an exception disproving the rule of Hollywood's conservatism? I think not, simply because he was not the innovator. The idea of putting a mag head in one of his cameras and using mag-striped film (commag) instead of comopt had already occurred to another party – significantly far from Hollywood and, indeed, the USA.

At a previous SMPTE convention, held in April 1955, a paper had been presented which revealed that the Germans had perfected the use of mag stripe film in the Auricons. This indicated that they were still thinking creatively about the magnetic recording technology they had pioneered in the 30s; it also revealed that they were being more creative about 16mm than were the Americans. Südwestfunk-Fernsehen, the TV station in Baden-Baden, had adapted all three cameras in the Auricon range by taking out the optical system and inserting a Klangfilm magnetic recorder instead. The station had not only these cameras but also projectors, kinescope or tele-recording (TV-to-film) devices and editing rooms all equipped to work with mag stripe. At the time of the report Südwestfunk had been using mag for two years, that is from 1953.[89] This is the earliest indication that I have discovered in the technical literature informing the Americans of new production uses for 16mm mag stripe stock. Until this revelation, the main applications for mag were seen to be quite specialised and limited to exhibition, as I have indicated above.

Bach and his partners were therefore simply following this German lead. Both Südwestfunk TV and Bach Auricon Inc. had taken a print stock and put it, not into a projector, but into a camera. At the 1956 SMPTE convention, Bach explained how he could either replace the optical sound elements in existing Auricons with mag or offer the cameras with a mag head fitted instead of the optical system. Either way the Auricon remained a single system device. It had recorded image and sound on one strip of film (comopt); now it recorded them on a combined strip of film and tape (commag). While this worked well enough for TV news the fact is that commag editing is as impossible as comopt editing.

In 16mm commag, the standard has the sound running twenty-eight frames ahead of the picture allowing the magnetic head to be placed well away from the film gate. Cut commag film and the first frame of soundtrack would be more than a second behind the first frame of picture. Just as a sepa-rate optical system was needed for full flexibility so a separate magnetic one was, too. But the TV news application minimised the difficulties this caused because it required little editing, especially of speech. The tendency to use very short quotations, sound bites, from interviewees meshed well with this technical limitation as did single-shot (or single-cut) reporter pieces to camera ('stand-uppers'). Thus, to edit in anything but a crude way required rerecording the sound from the original magnetic stripe on to a separate reel of audio tape formatted as 16mm film (i.e. with sprocket holes). This could then be run in perfect synch through the various editing and post-production devices and systems. This double system is termed 'sepmag'.

Despite the problems of commag, the Filmagnetic was a major success. The camera had been assured of this because CBS had been evaluating the modification even before it was officially announced and was able to declare the camera 'satisfactory'.[90] For the next fifteen years the Auricons 'domin-ated the TV newsgathering field'.[91] Needless to say, therefore, Bach attracted competitors. But the TV news people came to terms with their Auricons so effectively and were therefore so wedded to them that when manufacturers began to offer other commag 16mm systems, they were not successful.

At first, these competitors were in a rather improvised style and it is easy to see why the Auricon's dominance was not much affected. For example, the

British adapted the Arri St to use mag stripe. Rank Precision Ltd. did this by mounting the camera on a light-tight box that contained the magnetic heads, the camera base having been removed to allow the film to pass through this soundbox. The camera was then encased in a blimp. Clearly, portability was not an issue as the camera now became, in its blimp, about as big as a 35mm studio model; but it did not matter. Like the Filmagnetic, it was not designed to be used anywhere except on a tripod in fairly formal news situations.[92]

It took more than a decade for the first commag 16mm cameras designed from the ground up to reach the market. A Cannon single system was introduced in 1970 as was a sound version of the Beaulieu.[93] Even Paillard-Bolex attempted a design to compete with the Auricon. None of these cameras was any more successful than was Rank Precision lash-up. This was because commag's time had passed. Significantly, it was no longer the needs of TV news driving the technology. The impetus for next phase of change had moved on to other professional film-making quarters.

Supervening Necessity:
Stage 3 – 'A Breath of Fresh Air for Documentary'
As factual film production in 16mm for television and elsewhere became more sophisticated, it became more and more obvious that a sepmag system would have to be created with a camera completely separate from the sound recording device. This documentary push constituted the last (and least) element of supervening necessity transforming 16mm into a professional gauge.

Bach did not know his innovation was going to cause a major aesthetic breakthrough in documentary films. In fact, he seemed to be barely aware of the world of documentary as a potential market. This is almost certainly because, after the glory day of the 30s and the war, documentary had settled into a safe corporate-sponsored mode by the early 50s. It was scarcely a major area of activity and Hollywood equipment (including the Eyemo) was perfectly acceptable for that sort of work. In his initial sale pitch, Bach and his colleagues spoke of the camera being used for 'the television industry, as well as for educational and industrial films';[94] omitting all mention of documentaries.

He should have known better. The Germans had reported that they were using their adapted Auricons for documentary work. Moreover, as the American television networks were discovering the viability of documentary (albeit as much, if not more, for public relations rather than mass audience reasons), the post-war sponsored slumber was coming to an end. In 1957, for example, CBS announced they were thinking about copying the Germans; that is, giving up on 35mm and shooting documentary on 16mm.[95]

Although there is little evidence that they did so, it is certainly the case that they (and their rivals) made a lot of documentaries – still on 35mm. Magnetic sound had made synch shooting possible by removing the enormously cumbersome optical camera. That was advance enough and so, in consequence, network documentary production stills reveal the presence of 35mm cameras as late as 1963.[96] If 16mm were used, as far as the television companies were concerned, the Auricon as it had been developed for news work would do well enough. The basic style of documentary filming in either gauge was to shoot almost everything on a tripod, using (for example, in 16mm) an St or other silent camera for the bulk of the action and the Auricon for synch scenes and interviews – very much a continuation of the methods first developed by the newsreels to cope with the coming of sound twenty years earlier. For editing, the soundtrack was re-recorded on to 16mm magnetic stock.

This was not to be good enough, though, for a new generation of documentary film-makers who felt that these techniques, certainly in 35mm and even in 16mm, did not allow for real documentary observation. Richard Leacock had shot the last major work of Robert Flaherty, the man conventionally credited, because of *Nanook of the North* (1922), with the 'invention' of the form. This was *Louisana Story* (1948). Leacock was frustrated that every time a synch shot was required, camera fluidity was lost and rehearsals destroyed authenticity and spontaneity. In the 50s he increasingly wanted to do a heretical thing – carry the camera, not into war, but into any situation he wished to document and, moreover, capture sound at the same time. His early attempts to do this – in a New York jazz club or while following one of the last travelling variety tent shows in America – caused one of the pioneering pre-war American documentarists, Williard Van Dyke, to describe this footage as 'a breath of fresh air for the documentary'.[97]

The Auricon Filmagnetic was a massive step forward but for Leacock it still left much to be desired. As a result, he and the others involved in a group which formed around Robert Drew at Time-Life Films in New York and in Canada at the National Film Board began to adapt Bach's new machine to their own purposes. They were doing this within years of the Filmagnetic's introduction. The results were as curious as the Rank Precision blimped single-system Arri, but the effect they had on film-making was to be radical.

The Auricon was too heavy, at 26lbs, to be carried with any ease and therefore the body needed to be recast in a lighter metal. Doing this meant that it could now be carried more easily but it was still a square box, with the eyepiece mounted halfway up one side. To bring this to the eye required that the operator be tied into elaborate corset-like contraptions. The idea behind all this was, as Leacock wanted, that events, for the first time, should be more important that the filming of them. The idea was also that sound should be authentic and not added later and that poor lighting conditions should be as small a barrier to filming as possible. To this end, a portable (i.e. battery-powered) light of a sort that had been available to film-makers since before the turn of the 50s was sometimes fixed to the camera's top. Some direct-cinema proponents wished to avoid the use of film lights of any kind as being too intrusive. In this desire they were aided by the stock manufacturers. Black-and-white film stocks had been getting faster (that is, more responsive to low light conditions) throughout the 50s because of the needs of TV news and the fact that electronic cameras could operate competitively in very low levels. The Time Inc. group now took this a stage further by asking the developing labs to 'cook' the film; literally to process it at a higher temperature and/or longer time than was intended by the stock manufacturer. This produces greater sensitivity to low light but at the cost of increased grain. All these factors combined to create a grainy, hand-held, authentic-sound, go-anywhere style of film that was entirely new. Documentary had entered its direct-cinema phase.[98]

This new approach to documentary became the norm, even for mainstream TV documentarists. The latter did not follow the rules elaborated by the direct-cinema practitioners as regards non- (or minimal) intervention, but they nevertheless stole the synch sound, the available or crude lighting and, above all, the long hand-held take. Bach, responding to this activity, produced a Special Model CM 77 of the Pro-600 Filmagnetic with a lightweight body 'especially for documentary filming'.[99] It was otherwise not redesigned. The Auricon, created for TV news, now became, in both light and heavy versions, the camera that put documentary film onto a new footing.

Yet this was still not enough for the direct-cinema practitioners who adopted an almost evangelical tone when talking about the equipment. The grail that they now demanded was a lightweight sound camera specifically designed to fit on the human shoulder, something for which nobody in the sixty-five years of the cinema's history had ever asked before. They were, however, too marginal economically – dozens of film-makers at most as opposed to hundreds of TV stations each using more than one Auricon – to actually make it worth Walter Bach's or any other manufacturer's while to build a camera from scratch. The camera, when it came, was built in France on the back of military R&D to the order of an anthropologist.

I have already indicated that for the minority of (albeit extremely distinguished) anthropologists who did use film, 16mm had been an option from the 30s. This tradition was continued after the war by Jean Rouch at the Musée de l'Homme in Paris. Rouch, an engineer by training, presents himself as a naïve, instinctive film-maker. He admired the 16mm work of Mead and Bateson and tended to use film in a pure field-notes mode. It was years before he discovered editing. Along the same lines, there is a story that on his very first expedition to Niger he lost his tripod in a river and thereafter never took a shot with one again.[100]

Be all this as it may, the fact is that Rouch elaborated over a period of many years a very sophisticated approach to the problems of ethnographic film-making. Like Leacock he too wanted, for scientific reasons, the event to be more important than the filming. Slowly he also came to want to be able to get behind the event into its real significance and this required having his subjects talk. When in 1959 he came to make synch sound sequences, he too was appalled by the degree to which it slowed him down. He had also begun to put himself into his films as an earnest of their truthfulness.[101] By the late 50s the politics of anthropology were becoming extremely vexed. As the colonial empires collapsed into a number of independent states, Rouch determined to quit Africa to make a film about the strange tribe that lived in Paris. Aware that the Americans and Canadians were working with hand-held synch, he engaged the services of Michel Brault, a leading 16mm synch sound pioneer from the National Film Board of Canada, to help shoot this film, *Chronique d'un été*.

Rouch had also been discussing filming difficulties with the designer André Coutant. When Brault arrived in Paris in the summer of 1960, he was given the latest version of a prototype camera which Coutant had been working on for the previous couple of years. Using a small film mechanism he had made for telemetry purposes in connection with the French guided missile programme, Coutant was trying to perfect a self-blimped, that is, silent-running, hand-holdable camera with a wholly separate sound recording system. By 1960 the camera was not yet perfectly silent-running but it could be used with a light cloth blimp that did not really increase its size or impede its portability. All the *Chronique* production stills show it draped in cloth. Nevertheless, as Rouch wrote: 'Another advantage, the camera in its housing was minuscule. We could film in the middle of the street and no one would know we were shooting.'[102] This is scarcely surprising since one still shows Brault with the thing literally tucked under his arm.

Two years later the camera was ready to market. It was called the Éclair, 'The Flash'. In its final form, the weight of the lens was balanced by the weight of the film magazine which was shaped to sit on the shoulder. The motor was mounted below the lens and forward of the magazine at an angle to the lens/shutter plate so that it completed the shoulder-shape partially formed by the magazine. Professionally, this was seen as 'a major breakthrough in 16mm camera design'.[103] Given that the basic R&D for this camera had been paid for by the French government, Coutant had the edge on other designers. Instead of the documentarists' ideal machine costing more to develop than it was ever likely to recoup in sales, Coutant was able to recycle his military work to create a new product.

Coutant was also able to piggy-back a whole stream of developments in sound recording. These had allowed him to respond to Rouch's problem with a concept that separated camera and tape recorder. The Éclair was designed to be double system, with a recorder running in synch with the camera. Again, the Germans had shown the way. Before 1955 Südwestfunk TV had been shooting 16mm double system, as well as experimenting with adapted single-system Auricons:

> The picture is taken on 16mm film, the sound recorded synchronously on a separate 16mm full-coated film [i.e. sprocketed magnetic stock]. ... This type of picture includes all kinds of short subjects such as educational films, travel films, local or country-wide events, special interviews, etc. With these subjects the editor has time and freedom to produce a high-quality motion picture in which picture quality, editing rhythm and sound balance are essential and the superiority of magnetic sound recording becomes evident.[104]

However, the direct use of 16mm mag stock as an initial recording medium was not taken up anywhere else. Instead, $1/4"$ audiotape emerged as the industry norm. After initial recording, the $1/4"$ tape was dubbed onto 16mm magnetic film for editing. The significant technological issue facing designers like Coutant was to be sure that tape recorders were available that could render professionally acceptable sound but be as portable (i.e. battery driven) as the new cameras.

Such machines were readily available by the mid-50s, although one, the Minitape, was on the market as early as 1949.[105] At first it used miniature valves (tubes), as did the Auricons; later models used transistors. It could be synchronised with a spring-driven camera. Other portable recorders themselves had spring-driven tape transports, reserving limited battery power for the audio circuitry.[106] Not directed at amateurs, these were small location recorders specifically made for professional radio broadcasters and 'the fringes of missionaries, researchers and motion picture producers'. As late as 1959 it was still possible to characterise this latter market as being only sufficient to produce 'a scientific curiosity'.[107] Nevertheless, by 1956 no less than twenty-one types were on offer in the USA, most being made by small specialist firms. Some were very rugged. One, produced by the Amplifier Corporation of America, had a sort of driving wheel mounted forward of the tape reels whereby the spring could be wound. This became a standard machine for the US radio industry.[108] In Britain the equivalent portable for radio work, and subsequently for the earliest synchronised double systems, was the L2, made for the BBC by EMI.

At the same time, that is before 1955, a number of very small machines with battery-driven tape transport mechanisms were available, such as the Fi-Cord. Smallest of all, at $6^{1}/_{2}" \times 4^{1}/_{2}" \times 1^{1}/_{2}"$ and weighing only 2lbs, was the Tapette, described at a convention in 1954. This machine was so early that its designers were still addressing the issue of tape versus wire as the recording medium.[109] In some sense the magnetic element in the Auricon, in effect a miniature recorder, is in this line of development.

Obviously, a transistorised, fully electrical, battery-powered tape recorder posed no real design problems and Coutant had just the machine available to go with his prototype camera – the Perfectone.[110] It measured $12" \times 6" \times 2^{1}/_{2}"$. Although not specifically designed for movie work, it was demonstrated with a Camette blimped camera which had been modified to emit a synchronising pulse. Camera and recorder were connected by cable. The Perfectone recorded this pulse on a second track, the actual synch sound occupying the first. Subsequently the $^{1}/_{4}"$ tape could be transferred to fully coated 16mm mag stock using the pulse as a synchronising reference.[111] Although the principle remained constant, actual methods for laying down the synch pulse varied.[112]

With a Perfectone hooked up to his camera, Coutant had demonstrated that the ergonomic problem required no technological breakthroughs, just a simply breathtaking rethinking of the basic configuration so that the camera rested on the shoulder with the eyepiece placed at the eye. The camera was introduced in the US commercially in 1963 as the Eclair NPR, where it was brilliantly represented and was a 'resounding success'.[113] In my memory this was less the case on the other side of the Atlantic. The early NPRs had a tendency to jam because all the heaviest parts – lens, motor

84

and magazine – were attached directly to the most delicate element, the plate containing the shutter mechanism. Failure to leave anything but exactly thirteen frames of exposed film when preparing a magazine guaranteed a jam. Nevertheless, the Eclair, if not quite the grail because of these problems, in its ergonomic sensitivity and in its silence did fulfil the ideal design requirements of a new generation of documentarists.

As with the Auricon, the breakthrough camera created competition, and this time more swiftly. Arriflex responded in 1965 with the self-blimped Arri 16 BL. Less radical than the NPR, its body was essentially a standard Arri with a lens 'shroud' encasing the front of the camera to make it silent running. Motor and film transport mechanism were quietened and the eyepiece was also placed in a more ergonomically appropriate position half-way down the body. It still had a flat base to be balanced on the shoulder, but because it was more traditional and reliable than the Eclair, the BL made a considerable impact on the market.

The Auricon 'movement' was also mounted in a new body to produce, in 1971, the CP-16. This was similar overall to the BL configuration but rather boxier in design. By this time the Eclair itself had been modified into an even smaller body. This, the ACL, was introduced at the Photokina of 1970.[114] (Obviously it was the presence of these cameras that destroyed the chances of the single-system machines mentioned above which were being introduced at the same time.)

These self-blimped cameras had reduced mountings for prime lenses, that is, less than the old standard of three. The Eclair only had two mountings. On the BL, which only had one, changing the lens was, because of the silencing shroud, a comparatively laborious process; but this was no disadvantage because the camera came with a 10:1 12mm–120mm Angenieux zoom lens to replace the primes. The zoom lens became the norm for all documentary and news work, although in the earliest period it was more common to find camera operators using fixed-focus 10mm wide-angle lenses on their cut-down Auricons or Eclair NPRs. This was because the lens did not have a variable focus, allowing the camera operator to concentrate on framing and steadiness. However, follow focus was quickly reintroduced into the repertoire of skills and the Angenieux zoom became ubiquitous.

The Perfectone tape recorder also attracted a competitor. The Nagra, a machine around which much mythology has developed, became the standard for 16mm film work, not least because its designer, Kudelski, eventually specifically manufactured a model for that market, the Nagra III B, introduced in 1962.[115] None of his competitors was so accommodating. Weighing 15lbs, the first Nagra was introduced to the American market in December 1960, a year after the Perfectone.[116] The following May, at the SMPTE convention in Toronto, the National Film Board of Canada, a major site for researching the technology of portable synch sound, as Brault's career attests, reported on the use of the Nagra and the Pilot-Tone control (synching system), by then widely used in German television. The experiments in Canada had been going on since 1959 and the report pictured Nagras working with both an Arri St and an Auricon.[117]

Keeping the camera and the tape deck in synch now became the major issue occupying the ingenious and dominating film-making discussions. The film-makers did not want to be tied by an umbilical cord. By the early 60s numerous synching systems were in existence.[118] Some, like the Pilot-Tone, were commercially available but some were knocked together from such things as Bulova watches – very much in the spirit of Knight's 'ingenious amateurs'. Breaking the cord required no more than the demand. A transmitting crystal was mounted in the camera which sent the guiding synchronising pulse to a receiver on the tape recorder. Camera operator and sound recordist were thus uncoupled, greatly easing shooting.

Everything else needed was long since to hand by this time. Condenser microphones, especially the highly directional rifle mike, had been developed in the mid-50s.[119] Flatbed 16mm editing machines were available by that time. Motorised film synchronisers, another crucial editing room device, equipped with mag sound replay heads had been demonstrated in 1958.[120]

By the mid-60s the modern 16mm synch sound outfit was in place – Nagra with crystal control and an NPR or Arri BL. It was to take many more years, though, before Auricons or blimped Arri Sts (which used double-system with Nagras) or even more antiquated and curious combinations[121] were amortised and disappeared.

The breakthrough phase was now over. In the 70s, the tendency was to refine, automate and miniaturise the basic 16mm self-blimped reflex, with the NPR and the BL remaining the industry standards, although a sophisticated late arrival, the Aaton, enjoyed some success. By now the end was also in sight. The 16mm synch rig's heyday was to be a brief two decades. In the 80s the TV news business turned to electronic devices and the already quite small market for professional 16mm cameras lost its biggest component. By the mid-90s 16mm synch cameras, although by no means obsolete, were no longer subject to development. Film was everywhere under threat from advanced electronics, as is described in the next chapter; nowhere was that truer than of the realm of 16mm news and documentary production. The news was no longer 16mm's province and documentaries were also in the process of being lost to electronics.

The Rise and Fall of 16mm

The technological determinist view suggests that technological developments have a degree of autonomy – a life of their own. What the technology *can* deliver is what the technology *will* deliver and users will adapt. I am suggesting that, on the contrary, technology is always responsive to forces outside itself, with 16mm an excellent example of this. It could have been, from the outset, a professional gauge and could have developed as such, changing and growing with the cinema, instead it languished in an amateur ghetto. Its development owes little to scientific advances but a great deal to the propaganda needs of World War II, the regulatory needs of the nascent US television industry and the demands of a small group of documentarists and social scientists who had slowly become sophisticated about the nature of filmed evidence.

It is exactly the fact that virtually none of the technological developments upon which the professionalisation of 16mm depended was an actual advance in technology that makes 16mm such a good case study. In fact, all the advances had been to hand for years, if not decades, before they were put to use. For instance, there is the wide use of 16mm for projection in World War II on a projector introduced in 1932; or the 1918 proposal to produce high fidelity in a tape recorder, that is eventually taken up twenty years later. It is the consistency of this failure of technology to fix the timetable of what appear at first sight to be a series of technological advances that makes the 16mm case so rich. It is simply and solely the power of 'necessity', social necessities of various kinds, which either allows the gauge to languish or drives its diffusion forward.

The contention here is that 16mm is not unique in this regard. It is merely an excellent example of how such necessities, which are always grounded in the social, operate on a technological agenda. In the next chapter analogue high-definition television affords a case study of the complementary process – how the 'law' of the suppression of radical potential constrains the disruption any innovation might cause.

Chapter 4: The Case of HDTV

Lights, Camera, Inaction:
Hollywood and Technology

I have been arguing that new media technologies are introduced subject to pressures that take little or no cognisance of the viability of the technology itself. These pressures – cultural, social and economic – work either as Braudelian brakes or accelerators; or, as I term them, constraints and necessities. The proposal for a new analogue television standard of 1,125-lines, about which there was much professional and popular debate in the 80s, represents a very good case study of constraint – the 'law' of the suppression of radical potential – at work. Strategies were deployed to push the technology but the counter-strategies of those seeking to frustrate it were so effective that the system was virtually abandoned as a potential world transmission standard a little more than a decade after it was introduced to the market.

One from the Heart: Coppola's Strategy

On Tuesday 28 April 1981 Sony unveiled its latest wonder, production-line High Definition Television (HDTV) equipment in Tokyo. On hand to bless the range, fresh from shooting *One from the Heart*, was Francis Ford Coppola. He said he would never again make movies on 35mm film.[1] That spring, Coppola was having much to do with technicians. A month after the Tokyo launch, he was in Montreux, Switzerland, at the Twelfth International Television Symposium. There he explained to 2,000 of the world's top television engineers how he had used video as a sketch pad and database while doing *Heart*. More to the point, at this same meeting, he announced that he would shoot his next film, *Tucker*, entirely on video. It would be transferred to film only to make release prints – the final stage.[2]

By securing Coppola's support at these events Sony was sending a very precise signal about this technology. Sony engineers and marketers knew that what they were hooplahing early in 1981 as a substitute for 35mm film would stand or fall in film studios of the world in the hands of adventurous and influential film-makers like Coppola.

This was not, however, quite the vision of those who had done the basic research and development on the system Sony was trying to sell. HDTV in this analogue form had emerged from the research laboratories of the Japanese public broadcasting organisation, NHK, in the 70s. NHK's plans for it were, if anything, more ambitious than were Sony's but were rather different. NHK saw its HDTV as nothing less than a new universal world standard for television rather than a substitute for 35mm film.

Fifteen years on we can see than neither of these ambitions has been fulfilled and it is this double failure that makes analogue HDTV another interesting case.

Social Demands of Post-Industrial Societies: NHK's Strategy

Sony's HDTV picture was, electronically speaking, much like everyday North American or Japanese TV. It used 60-cycle electricity and produced two pictures which, when interlaced, made up one frame every thirtieth of a second. The signal was an electrical analogue of the original scene – a translation of light waves into a modulated electric wave. The major and significant differences lay in the number of lines scanned to make the picture and the shape, the aspect ratio, of the screen. Instead of the current US standard of 525-lines and a 4:3 screen, Sony demonstrated a system with 1,125 lines and a CinemaScope-style screen of 5:3 ratio.

As I have said, Sony had not done the basic work on this process. Around 1972 the firm had been cut into research and development, accomplished at the expense of the Japanese TV licence payers over the previous four years by the Advanced Television Systems Research Group, part of the NHK's Research Laboratories. Led by Takashi Fujio, it had been grappling with high definition since 1968. Technical objectives, such as how (or if) the system was to be delivered to the public, had been left vague; but the political importance of the agenda was clear.

NHK is modelled on the BBC and needs to renegotiate its contract with the Japanese government every five years, setting the level of the licence fee charged to the general public. It had become a tradition that the organisation would bolster its case by making a quinquennial technological present to the Japanese people. Teletext, for instance, was used to excellent effect in this context. Fujio's task was to provide a future bargaining chip. The fuzziness of the Fujio team's objectives is reflected in all its published early research papers. The purpose of the exercise, it was repeatedly stated, was to explore a new generation of television standards to meet the demands of 'a post-industrial society'.[3] Who was making such demands, apart from the NHK and its engineers, was unexplained.

Because of Japanese technophilia and high disposable-income levels, Fujio was not bound by the one constraint that has conditioned every technological advance in telecommunications in the West – compatibility. (Can the new signal also be received on the old equipment in the old way?) Fujio's concerns did not include the impact of his proposal on established producers, distributors and consumers of television. On the contrary, as a researcher in the world's electronic equipment production powerhouse he was working within a culture dedicated to obsolescence. He was therefore able to design a system incompatible with all existing television, including NHK's own, purchasing his widescreen 1,125-line picture at an enormous cost in bandwidth.

Bandwidth is the space occupied by an electromagnetic signal, such as TV. It is bandwidth that dictates that there be only thirteen channels in that part of the electromagnetic spectrum designated as VHF. The more complex the signal, the more bandwidth required. This is why there are hundreds of radio stations and only a few TV ones – pictures are more complicated to transmit than sounds.

But Fujio's HDTV was more complex than conventional television. It did indeed produce twice the signal resolution and a wider image, but at five times the bandwidth cost. Instead of the 6.5 million cycles per second (6.5 megahertz or MHz) required for the current US television picture, NHK's HDTV needed 30 millions of cycles (30 MHz). Put crudely, if – other things being equal – such a signal were to be transmitted on VHF, it would occupy the space currently taken up by five conventional TV channels. That would allow only two stations to broadcast in the VHF band. So goodbye, ABC and Fox. Goodbye BBC2 and Channel Four. Goodbye US independents and PBS. Goodbye thirty-six-channel cable (for only five services could be carried). In fact, goodbye television civilisation as we know it.

By 1979 NHK had successfully tested an HDTV transmission method – but not via a terrestrial system such as cable or mast. Instead an experimental satellite sending to a 1.6m receiving dish was used .[4] The signals to and from satellites are in the hundred of millions of cycles per second range (gigahertz: GHz), wide enough to accommodate the vastly expanded signal the Japanese were using. So bandwidth dictated the transmission mode and it is not too surprising that little notice was therefore taken of this event. Who, among the informed community of television engineers, could contemplate tearing up present terrestrial delivery systems for an increase in the quality of a signal that few if any were complaining about in the first place?

Broadcasters Must Maintain Faith: The Engineers' Strategies
In our culture, supposedly dedicated to the new and obsessed with techno-logical progress, constraint operates in a somewhat schizophrenic fashion. It often exhibits, as in this case, cognitive dissonance of a high order. Thus, even as many of them set about countering the threat Fujio's system presented to them, the world's TV engineers were full of praise for the design elegance of his accomplishment. They even gave him a medal for it (and NHK made him director general of its research arm). This cannot disguise the fact that as a basis for a new universal *home* TV system, the NHK proposal lacked, as they might say in Hollywood, 'legs'.

The first line of attack was on the compatibility issue. The engineers, especially in Britain and France, would not even talk about the NHK pro-posal until they had ascertained it could be 'down-converted' into current standards and cross-converted from NTSC (the current US TV standard also used by Japan) into PAL or SECAM (the standards used by the Euro-peans). In other words, could Fujio's system be ignored? The BBC summed up the engineering majority opinion: 'The broadcaster ... has to maintain faith with every generation of consumer purchasing equipment to a new standard.'[5] In the USA, the National Association of Broadcasters was just as direct: 'There are between 150 and 200 million NTSC-standard television sets in existence in the US market. Obviously, it would be preferable that a future US HDTV system would not leave the owners of these sets behind.'[6]

NHK threatened a complete upheaval at the end of which it would own the master patents on the production, transmission and reception equipment upon which the worldwide industry depended. Yet simply to take a strong negative view of this would expose the broadcasters to charges of self-interest, charges that their publics were being denied a technological wonder because of their own intransigence and backwardness. Compatibility offered a strong populist defence to these charges; but compatibility alone would not do. The technology itself had to be undermined. Since there is nothing so fatal to innovation as the suggestion that it has been prefigured, this sort of argument was also quickly adopted. The relationship of picture quality – sharpness – to bandwidth had been understood, of course, from the outset of television research. For example, the great Peter Goldmark of CBS, describing, in 1951, circuitry to improve the sharpness of the TV image at no cost, claimed that the device would 'give the *appearance* of having been transmitted through a system of greater bandwidth' (emphasis added).[7] It had also long been the proven case that better-quality pictures could be produced with more lines. Philips, for instance, claimed a 1,000-line performance for a black-and-white camera as long ago as 1952.[8]

For closed-circuit applications where the signal is not transmitted, such as in medicine, bandwidth was not a problem and the number of lines in the image could easily be increased. A 1,023-line standard was approved for such purposes in the USA in 1969, shortly after Fujio had started work in Tokyo.[9] Also in that year, Technicolor had announced a laser-based system to transfer film to tape at more than 2,000-lines per frame.[10] So, of itself, an 1,125-line picture was no big deal to the engineers.

Not only that. If there were a problem with current television it was not with overall clarity but rather in the systems' inability to cope with fast lateral movements within the image and the general resolution of fine detail – lagging, blurring and strobing. Had Fujio dealt with that? It turned out he had not. The point here is that hostile engineers began to ask questions of the Japanese system about which it had simply not been designed to take cognisance. It produced a television image breathtakingly wider and sharper than conventional pictures. Yet, when the engineering community had recovered its breath, it was prepared to attack on this highly technical question of lateral resolution.

The Fujio team's papers describe experiments using a 35mm still film transparency as the image source to be matched by their new TV system.[11] This can be justified because repeated subjective psychometric tests have found the image quality of such stills to be better than anything else. Although they are nowhere near the limit of human visual acuity, such images are perceived as being near the 100 per cent 'excellent' or 'window-on-the-world' category. In such tests 35mm motion picture film is also perceived as 'excellent' but as closer to the ninetieth percentile; 16mm images are judged 'very good' (85 per cent). US 525-line television as seen on a studio monitor is only 'good' (82 per cent). Well-tuned American home receivers are, at 72 per cent, just 'fair', and barely superior to Super-8 film (70 per cent).[12] The still transparency can therefore be justified as the benchmark for sharpness measured in terms of horizontal resolution; but, as NHK's critics pointed out, it also encourages the engineer to avoid confronting the lateral problems which depend more on vertical than horizontal resolution.

During the years of the Fujio team's efforts there was a growing body of technical opinion questioning the efficacy of measuring the sharpness of TV images solely by horizontal resolution. Ever since Zworykin interlaced the horizontal scanning lines in the early 30s, it had been taken as read that this doubled the quality of the image. It was not until psychometric tests were finally done in 1967 on TV images with the interlacing removed that it was discovered that the perceptual effect was far less than anticipated. Rather than doubling the perceived sharpness, interlacing, it was suggested, improved the image by only about 24 per cent.

Ironically, NHK researchers confirmed this comparative failure. NHK's psychometric tests, conducted in 1980, demonstrated that, perceptually, the 1,125-line system did indeed match the quality of 35mm motion picture film but it was also revealed, in a minor finding, that interlacing the HDTV picture had less than the conventionally anticipated effect.[13] Moreover, if interlacing two sixtieth of a second fields to make one thirtieth of a second frame actually only makes the image 24 per cent sharper, the effective perceived frame rate is not one-sixtieth but one-thirty-seventh – less than the twenty-four frames per second film standard.

All this was further ammunition with which to attack NHK. The NHK system certainly improved vertical resolution from a value of 338 (using a standard measure) in the current US TV picture to 731. But, the engineers asked, was this enough to ensure maximum quality of lateral motion rendition? And, a parallel question, did not Fujio's reliance on the old frame rate also represent a missed opportunity to correct the blurring and stroboscopic effects that mar the current image? Unfortunately, the trade press started to carry reports that, with the NHK system 'fast pans and tilts are not possible because of the lag problem'[14] – just as they were not possible with current TV systems.

Finally, these engineering questions, queries and attacks took the form of positive alternative suggestions, the most important of which centered on digitalisation. Many concerned with the quality of the television image in the 70s were convinced that interlaced analogue systems, although obviously capable of improvement, offered less promise in solving these inherent vertical plane problems than did digitilisation. Throughout the decade, engineers around the world worked to develop and agree to sampling standards for digitalising the TV signal. Digitalisation was a necessary part of the exponential expansion of video special effects capability in the late 70s and early 80s. MTV without digitalisation would have been impossible. Active work was underway to produce a digital videotape recorder. The design parameters of cameras and domestic receivers were being debated at technical conferences before NHK made HDTV the hot topic. Although digital signals also require large bandwidths, they can be compressed more easily than can analogue ones.[15] It was clear to many that digital was the wave of the future, and this mind-set was another factor in the attack on NHK's updated analogue system. Why propose such a thing just prior to the emergence of superior digital devices?

This reflex was quickly refined: wait for digital and in the meantime, by all means, improve existing transmission standards. This constituted the final rhetorical defence, if you will, against the NHK challenge. The current signal, without any real change, could be vastly refined. The average US television set displays about 250-lines only, instead of the 320 that should be received in the home. An enormous amount is lost in the transmission process and in the poor quality of domestic receivers.

In America, the studio monitor is perceived as being 10 per cent better than the home set, the difference between 'good' and 'fair'. In Europe the gap is less and even in Japan, which uses the same TV system as the US, domestic pictures are better. Certainly in the closed-circuit conditions of an American studio, the current generation of cameras is capable of 700/800-lines. Getting this video data out to the home involves updating transmission equipment at the stations, more stringent insistence that engineering standards be maintained, and electronic filters in the domestic TV set to clean up the incoming signal. This was an agenda for immediate action – in fact it was already being proposed in the mid-70s prior to any of the HDTV upheaval.[16] Beyond this, a whole slough of suggestions emerged proposing HDTV or near-HDTV signals within (or close to) the bandwidth constraints of the present systems. One solution was to break the analogue signal up into component parts – colour, brightness, sound. Each part is compressed and transmitted in sequential bursts – a bit of chrominance, a bit of sound, a bit of luminance, a bit of chrominance, and so on. This Multiplexed Analog Component (MAC) signal is reassembled into a whole image by a 'smart' TV set.[17] Such a system is being used for the European and Australian Direct Satellite Broadcasting (DBS) services to deliver a standard European PAL 625-line picture; but adapting it to a high-definition standard of over 1,000-lines is comparatively straightforward.

Other proposals also depended on 'smart receivers'. A dedicated chip, a frame store, could be used within the domestic TV to hold one complete frame of 525-lines. When, a thirtieth of a second later, the next frame arrives, the chip would meld both for display. This, progressive or sequential scanning, could produce 1,050-lines at no bandwidth cost and without the problems created by interlacing. Yet more proposals suggested signal folding, computer-aided processing, filtering and, most significantly, sampling and digitalisation to achieve the same sorts of results. Many were within the 6.5 MHz bandwidth and were compatible with current standards. Most were over 1,000-lines horizontal.[18] Some proposals were sophisticated enough to contemplate the individual treatment of each pixel within the frame to correct lagging, blurring, serrations and imperfections of all kinds – 'artifacts' is the rather curious technical term to describe these unwanted effects. Philips scientists hypothesising these 'movement adaptive techniques' said: 'Some people refer to this concept as HDTV. Because we think other visual improvements must also be included, we shall call it High Quality TV (HQTV)'.[19] Take that, Dr Fujio.

A meeting of the International Consultative Committee for Radio Transmission (CCIR is the French acronym) in Algiers in 1983 was so swept away by the 1125/60 NTSC proposal that it went so far as to mandate the *search* for a worldwide standard for HDTV. Sony were jubilant enough, despite mainly European doubts, to suggest that their equipment range was, as one of their sales pamphlets put it: 'A realisation of the broadcasters' mandate' for a world standard.[20] But three years later, the next CCIR meeting at Dubrovnik put 1125/60 NTSC 'high-definition TV on hold'.[21] Joseph Roizen, a specialist engineering observer for the American Institute of Electrical and Electronic Engineers (IEEE), summarised the objections as follows:

> *Technical.* Many of the CCIR countries that use 50-hertz colour television systems, like PAL and SECAM, felt that by its very nature the NHK system favoured the 60Hz field rate. This meant that it was basically incompatible. ...
>
> *Socioeconomic.* Great Britain, France, the Netherlands and West Germany ... were not about to let the Japanese follow their takeover of the home video-cassette recorder market by staging a coup in high-definition television.
>
> *Philosophical.* Many US proponents of the NHK system antagonised European and even Australian delegates at the CCIR plenary assembly by urging an immediate adoption of the standard.[22]

Five years after the initial demonstration in the West, NHK's push for a new world transmission standard was, in effect, over.

At lunch with Roizen, Fujio explained with sketches on a paper napkin how he had been using progressive scan himself ten years earlier but had abandoned it because he thought 1125/60 was better.[23] However, his own lab had already been revising that 1125/60 30 MHz NTSC decision by producing various sampling systems that gave near high-definition images within the current bandwidths. One of these was the basis of the NHK direct satellite service for Japan due to start in 1989. The 1125/60 proposal was not even going to be used for that purpose. In the event this service only began experimentally in 1989 with such a sampled system.[24]

The 'law' of the suppression of radical potential had worked. The 1125/60 30 MHz NTSC innovation was dead in the water not just as a world TV standard but even for the original purpose as laid out in Fujio's 1968 research brief. It had some effect, nevertheless. The NHK challenge focused and accelerated the somewhat desultory pace of research into improved TV systems. These anyway might have become invigorated as new TV display technology and the general saturation of the consumer market suggested a wholesale revision for marketplace reasons, but clearly NHK moved the whole business to the top of the agenda. This effect does not, however, run counter to my main contention which is not that constraints mean no change occurs; rather only that change will be contained. The constraints that killed off 1125/60 30 MHz NTSC simply indicate that HDTV, when it comes, will be less disruptive than that proposal required. In fact, HDTV is coming on stream now, slowly and with due deference to national sensitivities, time-tables and, most important of all, pre-existing technology.

All this, it need hardly be repeated, is without prejudice to the fact that the NHK system in the perfect circumstances of the trade-show demonstration was breathtakingly cinematic, instantly and obviously close to the quality of 35mm film that Fujio was trying to emulate. Had it been diffused, it would have revolutionised television. But, for all that it was not as revolutionary as it might have been, it was still too revolutionary to survive.

We're Behind Japan – Again: The Media's Strategy

The analogue HDTV story is also a perfect example of how technological-determinist hype operates. The press was first pushed to take note of high definition by Sony Corporation of America and enthusiasts such as Joseph Flaherty, the venerable CBS Vice-President for Engineering, whose techno-philia apparently blinded him to the obvious fact that the NHK proposal would mean the death of his network. Their theme was a simple one. As a *USA Today* story put it in 1987: 'We're behind Japan – again' and catching up will be hard to do.[25] The American press took notice of analogue HDTV almost exactly at the time the system was being shelved as a world TV stand-ard. I believe this was not an accident. For its supporters an appeal to the court of public opinion, especially in America, was vital if the CCIR Dubrovnik decision was to be overturned, albeit overturned only as far as the US was concerned.

This opened up a second possibility. American critics of the proposal also joined the chorus suggesting that the US was getting badly left behind. Although they obviously knew this was not the case, the possibility of sufficient hysteria being translated into considerable Federal research monies could not be ignored. (The model here was Sputnik which in the 50s caused a rattled Washington to free up money for education and research and development at an unprecedented scale.) The press began to understand that other HDTV systems were possible but took the researchers' point that catching up was in order. '"It's an object lesson in how the US is losing its ability to manufacture hardgoods in competition with the rest of the world," grumbles William F. Schreiber, director of advanced TV research at Massa-chusetts Institute of Technology' to *Business Week* in 1987.[26]

Although the economy did not allow a post-Sputnik flow of funds, the message did get through to politicians and the public. At the 1989 Consumer Electronics Show in Las Vegas, Norman Lent, a New York Republican Congressperson, said, 'Our future competitiveness in high-tech electronics could be at stake here.'[27] Thus it was that clearer pictures of *Lifestyles of the Rich and Famous* and the rest became critical to the nation's well-being. According to another Republican Congressperson, Don Ritter, at the same show, high-definition television was 'one of the most important inventions of the 20th century. This is a crown-jewel product.'[28] To be fair to these Repre-sentatives, the Pentagon had, a few days earlier, announced it would fund research into HDTV 'for a wide range of military applications'.[29] Not even the Sony Corporation of America could resist the possibility of pork-barrels being rolled out: 'Sony Seeks TV Grant from US: Debate Is Expected over Bid to Develop High-Definition Unit.'[30]

Needless to say, so eagerly did the press fall for this inferential frame of struggle, race and defeat that they totally failed to understand the opposing, and equally overstated, point of view that had emerged from the engineers in the second half the 1980s, i.e. that broad-bandwidth analogue HDTV represented no sort of breakthrough. It did – although it was flawed for the reasons the engineers stated and which I have detailed above. But the nuances of the actual technological situation were, quite typically, beyond the press. Thus *The New York Times*, reporting the 1989 transmissions in Tokyo said: 'Japan plans a quiet demonstration of how far ahead of other nations it is.'[31] That it was to be 'quiet' because HDTV was late, still experimental and cool towards the initial technological solution was not noted. Instead there was yet more talk of 'the gradual erosion of America's manufacturing base in several critical technologies'. (However, when this same *New York Times* reporter filed on the belated introduction of the actual HDTV service in 1991 he noted that 'almost no one was watching' and finally understood why the system would be skipped by the US.[32])

As the decade turned, the hysteria over HDTV lessened and Congress declined to free up any money for research. One would like to report that this constituted an object lesson in resistance to media techno-hype but, of course, this is not the case. After HDTV, we have been even more endlessly bombarded with similarly ill-grounded hysteria about the 'Super Highway' and the 'Internet'. I have no hesitation in making a prediction: when those 'crown-jewel' technologies are revealed as paste, something else will be hyped instead.

35mm Quality at 16mm Production Prices: Sony's Strategy
NHK's ambitions for its HDTV system as a world standard increasingly jeopardised Sony's plans for the same technology as a substitute for 35mm film. The 'law' of the suppression of radical potential prevented NHK from achieving its ambitions but it also left Sony in an ambiguous position. Plotting the fate of Sony's project offers further evidence on the nature of technological change.

Sony's tactic with the NHK system was made possible exactly because Fujio had chosen the 35mm transparency as the benchmark for his work. In this he was repeating television research history. Fifty years earlier the technical agenda of the original television pioneers was pegged to the quality of the 16mm image, which then translated into some 400-plus lines.[33] Matching 16mm was termed, in the 30s, 'high definition' in contrast to the 100 or less lines produced by mechanical scanning systems prior to 1930.[34] It was not that these pioneers wished to have the lesser standard; rather they simply knew 35mm quality was going to be impossible to achieve with the technology they had to hand. In the event, the bandwidths they determined as necessary for 400-plus lines proved capable of taking rather more – hence the US standard of 525-lines and the European one of 625. But it had long been known that the 35mm image would take 1,000-lines or 1 million pixels to achieve.[35]

Having known about the NHK's interest in high definition since 1974, the American Society of Motion Picture and Television Engineers (SMPTE) set up an HDTV Study Group in 1977. It included European and American engineers as well as Kozo Hayashi, the NHK researcher who was to conduct the psychometric and other tests on the Fujio team's apparatus a few years later. The Study Group began its work in 1977 and met for two years.[36] It concluded that any new standard would have three possible applications – in the home, in cinemas and in the film studios.

Of these, the Study Group thought that it was premature to attempt to define domestic HDTV but that it was clear that the home delivery of a high line number, very broadband system was going to be a long shot. So far, history is showing that to be the case. Cinema display, the group felt, was a stronger possibility technically. In fact, they felt that home HDTV would depend on audiences becoming used to the standard first in the theatres. But getting it into those cinemas needed considerable albeit clearly definable advances in display technology to become a practicality. (Also, although the Study Group did not consider it, the world's different TV systems and standards of electrical supply work against any electronically based international distribution system. Film has the edge for these reasons.) Either way the group's prognosis would appear to be on track.

As for studio applications on the stage and in post-production, the situation was different. These sites could be seen as closed-circuit environments and, without bandwidth considerations to worry about, the Study Group determined that 1,000 to 1,600 lines per frame with progressive – not interlaced – scanning would serve to produce electronic images capable of being transferred to film for results comparable with 35mm origination.[37] Although caught with the interlaced scan of the NHK system, it was this possibility that Sony was seeking to exploit in the 80s.

The company was helped in this by the film industry in Hollywood showing a growing willingness to work in a video environment. Even production people who insisted on the quality of film and shot film to get the 'film look' were increasingly transferring the images to tape immediately for all other finishing processes. As computer-assisted video editing and then pure computer editing (where the video material is converted into digital information) came on stream, the advantages of electronics in post-production were ever more apparent. It was becoming quicker and cheaper than film and could produce more sophisticated special effects.

By 1986 twenty-one prime-time US TV series were being originated on film but edited and finished electronically.[38] If the product is to be shown on television there is no reason to go back to film; and if a film print is needed, laser transfer technology is to hand. There has been a slow increase in the amount of prime-time non-studio programming shot electronically. The first two television cameras designed with the feature cinematographer in mind – the Ikegami EC-35 and the Panacam from Panavision – were used, for instance, by Universal to shoot a drama and a test episode of *Harper Valley*

PTA for the 1981 season.[39] This possibility, though, remained marginal because of the current TV standards; however, away from entertainment television, video has triumphed. All newsgathering and the majority of documentary and other location factual programming is now shot on video, with 16mm film (which used to be common for this work) fast becoming something of an endangered species.[40]

This, then, was the context for Coppola's attempts to use film and video synchronously on *One from the Heart*. Coppola's system allowed him constantly to 'preview' the film as he was shooting it with claimed savings, in terms of eliminated scenes, of $2 million.[41] Since Coppola still spent $24 million and the film bombed at the box office, costing him his Zoetrope Studio, this was a less compelling demonstration of the usefulness of the approach than it might have been. Nevertheless, such Zoetropean concepts as video viewfinders on film cameras to produce an instantly recordable and replayable image for continuity checking and other purposes are no longer exotic. Sony's position was therefore perfectly logical. If modern video, originally designed to replicate 16mm film, had in effect seen off that gauge in news and factual programming, why should not HDTV 1125, originally designed to replicate 35mm, do the same to *that* gauge – especially since the feature side of the industry was already half-way there in its adoption of video-editing for material originated on 35mm film?

Professional opinion was very impressed with the quality of the NHK 1125/60 signal and immediately saw its potential. The widescreen images glowed with a depth and vibrancy, especially if nothing much moved laterally. As I have said, the fate of the technology has nothing to do with its quality or even its failure to solve every last problem with the current television image. 'I believe', said one highly distinguished if somewhat overly technophiliac film figure, Douglas Trumbull, 'High Definition Television will seriously compete with, if not eliminate, 35mm film and even the present 70mm release formats.'[42] More importantly, HDTV was, as Sony wanted, quickly seen as a potential cost container: 'High-resolution has often been proposed for the production of motion pictures because it can reduce production costs.'[43] 'It offers 35mm film quality at 16mm production prices.'[44]

Sony would therefore seem to have been in a good strategic position were it not for NHK. NHK was driven by the need to give the Japanese TV licence buyer a technological reward and, if possible, secure Japanese patent dominance of the world's television. Substituting HDTV for 35mm would not fulfil either of these goals. Moreover, the more NHK pushed for the worldwide standard, the more the whole system was called into question – even as a production standard.

Sony had been roped into Fujio's research in 1973. The company was then perceived as having the best video-recording machines. Ikegami, with the best cameras, and Panasonic (Matsushita), with the best monitors, also became involved. Sony were at an important juncture. The company, hitherto only a consumer electronics manufacturer, was shortly to launch its first professional video equipment range, of course using current standards. Clearly, the NHK research opened the door to a wonderful possibility.

HDTV, effectively exploited, could give Sony a commanding lead in this new arena. The film studios were, anyway, moving towards video. Obviously the mismatched quality of 35mm and existing television was a drawback to the electronic penetration of that market. But what if television could match 35mm?

Sony unveiled its first-generation professional range, HDVS (for High Definition Videosystem), in 1981, Coppola by its side. By 1985 the firm was selling production installations at around $1 million per site. An expatriate American living in Paris, David Niels, bought the first one and began producing commercials profitably for French television. In New York, Barry Rebo established the Rebo High Definition Studio.[45] By 1987 there was enough to look at to justify a congress, which took place in L'Aquila, Italy.[46] All the masterworks of the new medium were on display – the early experimental shorts *Arlecchino* (1983) and *Oniricon* (1985) from Italy; the first feature, *Julia and Julia*, also from Italy, starring Kathleen Turner and Sting (with a lot of interlaced-friendly slow-motion[47]); the first mini-series, *Chasing Rainbows*, made for the CBC in Toronto. (The last was done strictly for financial reasons – CBC was always limited to shooting on 16mm.) Rebo brought a number of music videos and announced that he was working with Robby Benson to produce America's first HDTV feature, *Crack in the Mirror*. It was to be shot on tape and transferred to film for distribution, exactly Coppola's plan for *Tucker* announced six years previously.

By 1988 the National Association of Broadcasters (NAB) could report to its members that: 'A substantial amount of agreement exists between Japanese, Canadian and US interests on video production parameters for the 1125/60 HDTV system. ...The NHK 1125 production standard seems well on its way to being a "de-facto" production standard in many parts of the world.'[48] In this context, as we have seen, it was not really NHK's HDTV but Sony's HDVS, now developed to use even greater bandwidths, that was winning the day.

To get this far was a considerable achievement given that the 'film look' eludes the standard television camera for a number of very good and basic reasons. TV cameras typically operate best with the aperture on their zoom lenses one-third closed. Film cameras are normally set with apertures nearly wide open. The result is that the electronic image has greater depth of field. The sharp area, the plane the film-makers really want the audience to concentrate on, is thus more difficult to isolate with an electronic camera. The machine needs to have a smaller target plate, shorter tubes and to use single focal length (prime) lenses instead of the somewhat muddying zooms that are the electronic norm. There is also a problem about responsiveness. The whites in the image tend to burn out in a video camera. Film can cope with a greater range of light intensities.

Since Coppola, Sony has worked closely with a number of other film professionals to correct these problems. One major advance has nothing to do with the electronic technology. Just getting cinematographers to light in their usual style automatically goes a long way to giving HDVS 'a film look'. The lack of prime lenses could also be easily solved by simply making such lenses.

By the late 80s the Sony camera was available with a choice of nine zooms and two ranges, from Nikon and Fujinon, of five primes each – not quite the hundreds of lenses a cinematographer would have available for a film camera but exceptional for video. More complicated adjustments made the camera's performance to match the expectations created by film about depth of field and ranges of light intensity.

Sony also understood that it was not a single camera or even a single camera and recorder that would make the system attractive. Standard video did not effectively remove 16mm film until a whole chain of video equipment from camera through editing suite into dubbing was available. Portable cameras and videotape recording, for example, had not been enough to accomplish this by themselves in the 60s, so Sony produced a wide range of ancillary equipment for HDVS, including digital videotape recorders, monitors, widescreen display projectors, and switchers. Most critical were two different systems for transferring the taped image to film and machines for 'down-converting' HDVS into current TV standards. By the late 80s, the cameras retailed for $169,840 each. An eighteen-inch monitor was $11,750. The projection TVs started at $67,000. The videotape recorder was $202,160. By 1992 the camera was priced at $308,000.[49]

Nevertheless, despite all this success, Sony's HDVS ship was in danger of foundering in the wash of the wreck of NHK's HDTV world transmission standard. The engineers working on compatible advanced (or enhanced) TV systems argued that it was absurd to have 1125/60 2-1 interlaced as a production medium and 'down-convert' it to any number of potential rivals – 1025 Sequential Scan, for instance. ('Down-conversion' would then have to occur between two high-definition systems.) Again the Europeans, especially the British, French and Germans, were the most vociferous objectors.

After Dubrovnik, Sony spokespeople learned to be circumspect about the differences between their agenda and NHK's, and were at some pains to maintain a certain distance. Larry Thorpe, HDVS product manager in the US, for instance, at the NAB annual convention in Las Vegas in 1988 pointed out that Sony were so comparatively uninterested in HDTV as a home delivery system the firm was some years behind its rivals in the design and production of domestic receivers for the Japanese market. Nevertheless, Sony found itself perforce involved in the politics of international television technology. In addition to the usual glossy brochures for the gear, a series of communiqués started to appear. Two years after Dubrovnik, Communiqué Number 3 stated: 'Despite recent statements to the contrary in some international broadcasting circles, the real possibility of achieving a unified single world standard for HDTV production has by no means disappeared.'[50]

Sony were boxed into a rather difficult corner. A measure of acceptance was achieved in Japan and North America but the immutable laws of physics were allowing others to produce systems very close to the one Sony was selling that would be directly usable in the real world outside the studios – that is to say, compatible systems capable of 35mm quality in the studio and also capable of transmitting such quality to the HDTV home, whenever that came into being, without conversion. Sony were caught backing the least elegant electronic solution to the problem of high-definition TV. There was really only one hope: Hollywood, initially in its TV prime-time factory mode and then subsequently for all its operations, would have to take HDVS 1125/60 to heart. Were that to have happened then other film studios around the world would have had to follow. Sony would have won the gamble.

Give Me One Good Reason to Change: Hollywood's Strategies

In Hollywood parlance an 'apple box' is a species of building block used for raising people and/or equipment to a desired height.

> Several years ago a grip discovered that by cutting the handles of an apple box in an off-center rather than a centered position, they could be carried two at a time with one hand, instead of one at a time as was previously done. This idea was debated for a time and is slowly coming into acceptance. ...When you pick up apple boxes a thousand times a day during the long working conditions of a dramatic production, you want to know that the movement of the handle from its traditional position is not going to create more problems than it will solve.[51]

The parable of the apple box was offered to the 1984 SMPTE Television Conference on new technologies by Harry Mathias, cinematographer and senior consultant to Panavision. 'The motion picture industry is actually,' he claimed, 'fiscally and technologically conservative. ... The film industry unlike the video or computer industry does not possess a "Gee Whiz" attitude towards new technology, but more a "give me one good reason to change" attitude.'[52]

Mathias mentioned the Moviola, the industry-standard film editing machine, as another good example of this Doubting Thomas stance. The machine, drive shafts and belts exposed, looks like a species of 30s high tech – which it is. It has an alarming tendency arbitrarily to destroy film. The flat-bed film editor, a better, more efficient, user-friendlier and gentler alternative, has existed since the 50s yet it never totally replaced the Moviola. These are still to be found even in the era of ubiquitous computer-based electronic editing systems.

In part, the persistence of trickier and less efficient techniques and machinery has to do with the mysterium of the crafts involved. The skills of a film editor were seen to be, at least in some measure, bound up with her or his Moviola-taming abilities. Although the skills and talents needed to put a sequence of moving images together effectively were clearly understood not to be limited to machine-minding, nevertheless it was almost as if the industry believed that any fool could run a flat-bed. However, industry conservatism is more systemically rooted than the unwillingness of a highly skilled labour force, conditioned to believe in its own talents if not artistic creativity, to embrace change. As we have seen, Hollywood's bosses have also used technology, either because of its complexity or its cost or both, to limit competition by creating barriers to entry.

Hollywood, as an industrial system, has only once retooled to the extent that the adoption of HDTV would now require and that was with sound. Sound therefore affords a good model of how the studios react to such challenges.

They Could Not See the Sound: Hollywood's Strategies (1)

The change to sound offers poor omens for HDTV. To be brief, more than six decades were to pass from the birth of the cinema before modern sound recording techniques became the Hollywood norm. That is the time it takes for tape recorders to make it onto Hollywood stages. Magnetic soundtracks for exhibition purposes were in use some years earlier. These delays are in themselves a clear indication of the correctness of Mathias's view of the inherent conservatism of the industry.

I say this despite the fact that it is customary to look on the period of the late 20s as an era of near panic and rapid change as the film industry adopted sound. Yet this view requires that all the previous sound film systems be either ignored or treated as prototypes that did not quite work. The problem about this approach is that what worked in the late 20s, especially the Vitaphone system, was exactly comparable to some of these earlier formats. Even the optical sound system that was eventually adopted required no break-throughs to become 'the invention'. All the competencies involved, from the wave theory of sound and light to the existence of the thermionic tube and the microphone, were to hand long before. The idea of putting the sound in a strip down the side of the film dates, as I pointed out in the previous chapter, from 1909.

It seems to me not unreasonable to see this as the production wing of the industry simply laying off the cost of providing sound on to the exhibition wing and for nearly a quarter of a century finding no reason to adopt or develop technologies that would shift those expenses on to their shoulders. It was only when comparative fringe players demonstrated improved market shares and profits even after absorbing those same costs that the industry as a whole was forced to follow suit. Even then, the usual patent problems, again a clear indicator that nothing really new was involved, slow the adoption of a final standard for some years. Finally, as I have described above, the whole cycle repeats itself with optical sound now the source of inertia vis-à-vis tape just as live music had been the source of inertia vis-à-vis optical sound.

It will be objected that the delay in adopting tape was quite reasonable, at least until the start of World War II, because the technology was not really available since the quality of magnetic recording was still poor in the early 30s. It was not until researchers at the German State Broadcasting Service corrected this that tape became a real alternative. But my point is that the supervening necessity of recording the Nazi leadership's speeches caused this breakthrough – not any advance in science or even in basic technology. What German technologists did for Goebbels in the early 40s, American technologists could have done for the Hollywood studios a decade earlier, had they been asked so to do and supported. As it was, it took more than twenty-five years from this point, or thirty-five years from the start of the sound film era, for a magnetic recorder to make it onto a Hollywood stage and for the last fifteen or more of those years the Nazi technology was freely available in America and used increasingly in the broadcast industry and even in the home.

In the early 50s, another sidelined technology, widescreen systems, which had also been some decades in the offing since they had been demonstrated as viable in the 20s and 30s, was finally introduced. These systems, Cinerama (1952), Cinemascope (1953) and Vistavision (1954), all had provision for stereophonic sound and came to rely on prints with magnetic sound.[53] But this application was for exhibition only. Production of stereo sound, of course, did not of itself need magnetic recording. *Fantasia*, for instance, had been made in 1940 with stereophonic tracks on standard 35mm optical stock. Despite magnetic tape's clear technical superiority for recording the multiple tracks stereo demanded and its use for widescreen exhibition, almost another decade was to pass before, finally, a Hollywood feature's sound was recorded on to magnetic tape. *Geronimo*, directed by Arnold Lavin for Paramount and starring Chuck Connors, became the first film to have a magnetically recorded track – in 1962.[54]

The hostility of Hollywood to what was by then a well-established film technology in television and widescreen created what John Belton calls 'a frozen revolution'. It constitutes a classic example of how social attitudes about the nature of a particular task operate within broader economic forces (such as amortisation costs) to suppress the disruptive potential of new technologies: 'Most editors would have nothing to do with magnetic sound. The great complaint was that they could not see the sound modulation on the magnetic film, and they were in the habit of using the modulation on optical sound film as an index of synchronisation.'[55] When finally the industry started to use magnetic sound, the first tape machines it adopted weighed 64lbs, were described as 'lightweight', but were mounted in the same large trucks as had carried the optical sound cameras. As little as possible was changed.[56]

Technicolor: Hollywood's Strategies (2)

As with sound, so with colour.

Like sound, colour was present from the beginning of cinema, as I have described in Chapter Two. Hollywood moved from the widely diffused technique of hand tinting to tinted stocks. This started to shift control over colour from the producers to manufacturers such as Eastman, but at the same time it also provided the beginnings of a specialised system of reproduction which afforded the producers a measure of protection. The implicit logic of this tendency then became clear with the triumph of a highly specialised and highly controlled colour system – Technicolor.

Eastman's modern tripack colour film, even though the format marketed gave the company a monopoly over developing, used ordinary cameras. This threatened the level of control exercised by Technicolor with its patented camera. But this was not allowed to become a reason for abandoning

Technicolor – on the contrary. Once more the use of a very complex, expensive system was a source of inertia. This was despite the fact that it was Technicolor, not the studios, which controlled the production of prints. It was Technicolor's technicians, not studio employees, who operated cameras and Technicolor's 'Color Directors' or 'Consultants' who dictated, as often as not in the interests of compensating for the deficiencies of the process, the overall design of a film, including costuming, lighting and elements of the *mise en scène*.[57]

The reliance on Westrex sound made Hollywood a prisoner of the phone company; the reliance on Technicolor made it a hostage to Technicolor's owner, Dr Kalmus. In both cases, though, the relationship enshrined implicit protection against competition. So, just as it remained largely loyal to Westrex, Hollywood also stuck with Technicolor. Tripack dye-coupler film stocks were not, of themselves, enough to break Technicolor's hold.

Hollywood's conservatism sustained the status quo until eventually Technicolor became something of a victim of its own success. As more and more films came to be made in colour Technicolor was overwhelmed with work. It became a bottleneck.[58] This could not and indeed did not persist. The monopoly collapsed and by the 60s, modern Kodak materials were the industry standard in North America, Britain and throughout most of the rest of the world. Technicolor was reduced to being just another chain of labs handling them.

The fact remains that the industry could have had a far more effective, cheaper and technologically more elegant colour system decades earlier than it did. It chose not to.

It will be objected here that complex patent agreements between Technicolor and Eastman Kodak meant that Kodak 35mm was not really available. But this, I would argue, is to mistake symptom and cause. The unavailability of Kodak 35mm motion picture stock clearly was not a function of technology. You could buy it formatted for your Leica or your 16mm movie camera. The failure to package a version of it for Hollywood was a symptom of the operation of the 'law' of the suppression of radical potential rather than a technologically determined cause of the situation.

Too Grainy for Projection: Hollywood's Strategies (3)

All of this raises a basic question about the industry's most basic standard, 35mm film. As I have described in Chapter One, 35mm developed from the natural, if culturally determined, tendency of early researchers to work with film strips in familiar widths. Edison, the Lumières and Eastman settled on 35mm – as acceptable to Anglo-Saxon sensibilities as it was to the French. And then the usual story. First were the legal difficulties in the form of a patent war and then inertia ensuring that 35mm became the standard. Other possibilities, notably wider gauges to aid theatrical projection, were suppressed and so were stocks narrower than 35mm, despite the fact that they would be cheaper to use and more accessible to producers. Although it was obvious too that they would produce less effective images in the theatrical context (as did 35mm vis-à-vis 70mm), if refined they might have been usable in all but the biggest cinemas. In fact, today's 'substandard' (as the significant term-of-art has it) 16mm stock is perfectly adequate for halls seating hundreds.

Even at the outset, when substandard stocks would clearly not work in the vaudeville theatre setting, they nevertheless did appear and quickly – 17.5mm, 28mm, 22mm, 21mm, 15mm and 11mm were all tried.[59] However, the patent wars ensured that professional use was, within five or six years, limited to 35mm. Interest in most of these alternatives was limited to their potential for amateurs.

The research and development of a narrower stock was (as was explained in the last chapter) thus sidelined into an attempt to open up a market for amateur movie-making. Its 'professionalisation' was to take decades because the research and development needed to improve sub-35mm stocks to anything like the standard theatrical distribution demanded was inhibited. For the mainstream industry, secure behind the economic barrier 35mm represented both in the studios and the theatres, to ignore the smaller standard made sense. Theoretically, 16mm threatened the mysterium of production and the oligarchic exhibition situation and, like magnetic tape and dye-coupler colour film stocks, it was ignored by Hollywood.

It is clear that as far as technology is concerned there are here many roads not taken by Hollywood. And this was the culture into which Sony was proposing to introduce a technological change at least as great as any described in this book.

A Man and His Dream: Coppola's Strategy Revisited

Francis Ford Coppola did not make *Tucker* next, as he had promised his Montreux audience in 1981. And when he did make it, in 1987, it was not shot on video. The disastrous reception of *One from the Heart* cannot be blamed on the technology used to produce it but on the quality of the piece itself. By the time *Heart* went into production, Coppola was being forced to bet Zoetrope on its success – not an ideal situation in which to experiment with new production techniques. For instance, the 'electronic stuff' he brought onto the lot cost a reported $800,000. It did not help the film. The studio was lost.[60]

Coppola recovered his own career by returning to directing pictures. Of course, since he no longer owned the store he was not allowed to stock it with video goodies. He was forced to work in a technologically conventional way except insofar as the techniques he had been using at Zoetrope, such as the video viewfinder, had become generally accepted. He eventually got to make *Tucker* in 1987 with the help of his old friend George Lucas.

Tucker: A Man and His Dream chronicles the saga of a real-life visionary designer, Preston Tucker, whose scheme for a revolutionary car is scuppered by Detroit in the late 40s. The picture was widely received as a autobiographical statement about Coppola, Zoetrope and the video experiments of *One from the Heart*. One film magazine described it as: 'Tucker – the true story of a maverick car designer so revolutionary he was forced out of business. (Sound familiar?)'.[61]

The real Tucker's difficulties stemmed from a faulty analysis of the auto industry and a too naïve belief in the efficacy of the better mousetrap. Coppola was guilty of making the same sort of mistakes about movie-making. Such errors in all technological fields are common and stem from a failure to consider the social, cultural and economic context when assessing a new technological option. Disruption will be minimised at all costs. The least significant factor in making technological assessments, as Coppola and Tucker and many others have learned to their cost, is the actual technological possibility itself. That a thing can be done means very little. Coppola's groping for an integrated film-making process is a powerful example of this.

To go from script to final film within a single computing or computer-aided environment, allowing every technical and creative department access to the entire process, is now a very real possibility; but actually to push such a system into operation is to over-design. The film's accountants, for instance, simply do not have to see the designer's floor plans. They couldn't understand them. The writer does not need to see the accounts. She couldn't understand them. The videotape of the rehearsals doesn't have to be laid over the production designs; the final shot can be stored apart from the screen-test footage. So why do it? What within the cultural infrastructure, the deep-rooted socialisations of movie professionals, would suggest there are real benefits in creating such fluidity?

And why, if one accepts that such computer/video interfaces would save money, would the film industry buy into them? Barriers to entry are socially, politically and economically critical and critically depend on complexity and expense. There might be little advantage in seeking any processes that lower the cost and therefore also lower the barriers to competition. Why introduce technologies and techniques that could, say, wipe out the difference in production values between a theatrical film and the made-for-TV feature? All media might well be capable of convergence in the way Coppola was suggesting; that doesn't mean much is gained by their converging.

Preston Tucker, at least in Coppola's vision of him, is a man dedicated to saving lives by bringing essential safety features into cars. It is hard to find a similar compelling justification for changing film-making procedures. And it is too easy to dismiss the movie people resisting change as the usual mindless Luddites. After all, video and computing support is already present in the process. It is where the industry needs it to be and where it can be contained. Almost without question it will slowly reach into other areas, again as long as disruption to underlying social and especially economic formations can be contained. However, overall, video's radical potential to disrupt the industry has been and is being suppressed. New technologies will come (are coming) but they will be (are being) conformed to the old. Hollywood will survive (is surviving) them.

This slow progress applied to Sony's HDVS. In the mid-90s, fifteen years after the Montreux launch, Hollywood was still essentially a 35mm town and, despite the encroachments of video into post-production, film is still not really being challenged on the studio floor or in the cinemas. On TV there is a slightly greater degree of flexibility with enhanced 16mm (Super 16) now seen as a viable alternative to 35mm, but this flexibility does not often extend to include the possibility of HDVS. In news production, film is certainly a thing of the past and it looks to be nearly so in documentary – but, again, in neither case is HDVS used instead. It is video in all its current standard guises which has slowly over the last quarter of a century taken over.

Hollywood has not embraced Sony's HDVS as it had previously embraced Westrex and Technicolor. Westrex and Technicolor contributed to the uniqueness of the Hollywood product. HDVS, despite the cost of the equipment itself, does not do this. It does not afford the sort of protection those technologies had brought. On the contrary, it was actually dangerous from this point of view because it encouraged the erosion of production values by threatening the distinction between the theatrical feature and the made-for-TV movie. In a world of eight or even nine figure feature film budgets, there is little point in going for '35mm quality at 16mm prices'.

The fact of the matter was that, in their 1980s forms, HDTV and HDVS brought obvious, clear-cut, real-world advantages to the Japanese only. The supposed benefits of better TV pictures for the general public sound more like empty rhetoric than expressions of real need which had to be met immediately – as NHK now knows. The promise of 35mm production values at 16mm prices was never a major plus for an industry conditioned to seeing expense as protection – as Sony has discovered. And, anyway, with such high start-up costs, how real were the savings?

The centre rather than the offset handle on the apple box. The Moviola rather than the flat-bed editing machine. Optical sound rather than magnetic. Technicolor rather than Kodachrome. 35mm rather than 28mm. And film rather than HDVS – for one final very good reason: HDVS was never going to be more than a way station on the road from film to video rather than the end of the road itself. The end of the road is 4,000 or so lines, the limit of human visual acuity, and digital ... and holographic.

And this is still some way off (as I point out in the next chapter).

The Five-Year Syndrome: The Technophile's Strategy
One would never get such a sense of measured progress from the technophiles. In 1981, as NHK and Sony unveiled 1125/60 HDTV to the world, there were immediate pronouncements as to how quickly it would triumph. Normally, the time span envisaged for a technology that already exists in the metal, as in this case, is five or so years. True to this rule, Joseph Flaherty pronounced that the development 'had brought high-definition television within the grasp of the consumer by 1986'.[62] The consultants Browne, Bortz and Coddington of Denver conducted a study and predicted that 'HDTV service to theatres might be a likely viable market as early as 1985'.[63] A decade after these dates, a few wealthy Japanese are the world's only HDTV consumers and no cinema anywhere has given up on film in favour of high-definition television.

Our amnesia about the history of technological developments will, however, most likely work as it usually does. When, sometime in the early decades of the next century, a fully compatible HDTV system is finally introduced and begins to be diffused, there will be much talk, as there usually is, of how swiftly this change is come upon us. Of course, by that time it will have been more like fifty years since Takashi Fujio began his researches. It is already over twenty-five. I attribute these delays to the 'law' of the suppression of radical potential.

Chapter 5:
The Case of the Third Dimension

Where Is Holography?: Necessities and Constraints

Given our fundamental addiction to realism, there is no underlying reason why a true three-dimensional motion picture system should not achieve a cultural fit and be diffused. But where is such a technology? Is it still in the ground of scientific competence? Is the idea articulated? Do the prototypes exist? Are we just waiting for supervening social necessity or are forces at work to suppress diffusion? In short, has true 3-D moving-image technology been invented yet?

From the Stereoptican to *Bwana Devil*

It seems safe to assume we have always known why we see solids. Certainly, what by now must be a familiar cast of great savants ('the usual suspects'?) figures in the standard accounts. In antiquity, Euclid and Galen provided physiological explanations based on an understanding of binocular vision which were repeated by della Porta; and Da Vinci in the notebooks explained why a single painted image did not produce an impression of three dimensions. Jacopo Chimenti, a sixteenth-century Florentine, attempted to produce stereoscopic pictures by making double drawings from slightly different angles.[1]

Binocular telescopes were constructed by 1608 and used essentially for military purposes until Voitgländer manufactured the first 'opera glasses' in the 1830s. (It could be that theatrical gas illumination, which did not have the same profound effect on acting style at the beginning of the 19th century that the introduction of electric lighting was to have at its end, nevertheless so much improved stage illumination that it was for the first time worthwhile seeing things in detail.) This line of development went on to produce binocular microscopes for science and, thanks to Zeiss technicians in 1899, range-finders for photography and, of course, the military.

Such devices locked the eyes into a position where it was also possible to create stereoscopic illusion. Sir Charles Wheatstone produced 'mirror stereoscopes' which did this using simple outline patterns in the 1830s. With photography, it became much easier to create detailed images having slightly different angles of view and this was done with daguerreotypes in a double-lensed camera by 1846. These were viewed through a stereoptican. Queen Victoria was amused by this device at the Great Exhibition of 1851 and the subsequent introduction of the wet-plate process, which made the mass production of stereographic photographs possible, fed something of a vogue in the mid-decades of the century. The realism of the illusion was of a piece with the basic realism of photography itself. Stereoscopes 'fitted' and persisted in this form into the last third of the 20th century, for example, in the popular optical toy, the Viewmaster.

Since three-dimensional photography was so well established, it is scarcely surprising that repeated attempts, some hundreds of them, have been made to establish three-dimensional movies over the cinema's first century.[2] Before 1900, for example, Friese-Greene had patented a stereo-scopic movie system to be viewed through a stereoptican. Motion picture devices such as the Mutoscope peep-show machines were readily adapted for binocular use but not the Cinématographe. Meshing stereoscopes, which permitted only one person at a time to view the effect, with the vogue for projected images was harder. However, proposals had already been made in the 1850s by W. Rollmann and J. Ch. d'Almeida for solving this problem with colour-coded images.[3] If one were, say, red and a second green, providing viewers with complimentary colour-coded glasses would allow a number of people to see the illusion simultaneously. The first people to don the red/green glasses did so sometime before 1858 in order to view d'Almeida's projected stereoscopic slides.

If we discount the wide curved screen systems (including Cinerama and Imax) as being scarcely stereoscopic, then only once has even a modestly successful 3-D system not involved glasses of one sort or another. During and immediately after World War II in the Soviet Union, when a feature-length version of *Robinson Crusoe* was made, a complex 'integral screen', a slated or prismatic variant on the lenticular principle, was used. Lenticular stocks, it will be recalled, embed slivers of glass into the film; lenticular 3-D systems embed glass or mirror shards into the screen. The Russian system, technically a 'parallax stereogram', needed no glasses but was generally held to be less effective than those that did use them. Nevertheless, five showcase theatres were equipped and were still in operation in the mid-1950s.

In the West, repeated fads have suggested, if only to the entrepreneurs concerned, that a 3-D revolution was at hand. The earliest movies to use the red/green glasses had been demonstrated in 1909,[4] but the first real upsurge of interest occurred in 1922/3 with a second peak in 1936. One of the systems displayed in 1922 even allowed for a degree of interactivity: 'By looking through the red glass, the viewer saw a different scene from the one he saw when looking through the green side. The viewer himself could decide whether he wanted a sad or a happy ending by closing either his left or his right eye.'[5]

At the New York World's Fair in 1939, a variant method was used which relied not on red/green filters but on light polarisation to separate the two images. The audience still had to use glasses but colour was now possible. This same principle, aided by devices to lock the cameras together which emerged from missile tracking technology,[6] was revived after the war and was a success at the Festival of Britain in 1951, when two Norman McLaren cartoons astounded audiences, and during the 1953/4 3-D boom – from the release of *Bwana Devil*, which was an unexpected hit, to the failure (at least in 3-D) of *Kiss Me Kate* , *Dial M for Murder* and *Miss Sadie Thompson*.

A polarisation filter transmits light which is vibrating in just one plane and the idea of utilising this phenomenon to produce stereoscopic images was first made in 1891. If the two stereoscopic images are arranged so that one is transmitted through the filter in a plane perpendicular to the other, then a pair of filters, mounted in glasses, can be constructed to receive each image separately. The eye/brain then melds the two images to produce a stereoscopic effect. Edwin Land demonstrated a method for producing such a light polarisation material by treating a clear plastic in an iodine solution in 1936. He marketed it under the trade name Polaroid and it was used in a New York 3-D show in 1939 and thereafter, including a number of still-born television experiments in the 50s.

In our model, we can consign the understanding of how we see stereoscopically and the development of light polarisation materials to the ground of scientific competence. All the devices and systems for creating three-dimensional effects from the stereoptican to the parallel stereogram and the 'Natural Vision' polaroid method used for *Bwana Devil* can be classified as precursor devices and systems, prototypes of a dead-end kind. They are rather like mechanical scanning for television or, better, toy-like string 'telephones' which enjoyed a fad as 'lovers' telephones' in the decade before the electric telephone proper was developed. The technology works but not quite well enough. Perhaps most importantly, none of these stereoscopic methods offers true three dimensions but rather a 3-D illusion since each viewer sees the same angle on the scene wherever in the auditorium they sit. They feed our addiction for realism but leave it somewhat unsatisfied. As such, they constitute another element in the ground of scientific competence, one constantly revisited by successive entrepreneurs. (For example, in the mid-90s, the large screen system Imax began offering 3-D movies with glasses once again. Until something better in three dimensions comes along it seems as if the glasses, or the lenticular screen, will always be with us.)

Nevertheless, by playing with light waves, as Edwin Land had done in the 30s, it is possible to achieve true stereoscopic representation. Holography, as the system that creates such images is called, has been an established technique in some fields for more than three decades.

From the Interference Hypothesis to the Interferometer

I have positioned the development of stereoscopic image-making in the same entertainment tradition that produced the cinema and television; but, in fact, the real impetus for developments subsequent to the stereoptican came from elsewhere. The range-finder – or stereotelemeter – of 1899 produced a series of applications that had nothing to do with leisure. Stereotelemeters allowed for the measurement of the depth of clouds and other distant terrestrial objects as well as astronomical observations. These devices were in a line of scientific instruments designed to measure and inscribe reality. (Photography was initially also regarded as such a technology.[7]) They were less technologies of seeing than technologies of measuring. Even the essentially 'trivial' stereoptican was used in this way. For instance, as early as 1866 a series of images of a solid conic section were produced to create a stereoscope of the otherwise opaque interior of the cone. Most importantly it was realised that a stereoscope of an original object could be compared with actual copies and imperfections revealed. This was done for testing patterns in carpets or to distinguish counterfeits of coins.

The research agenda that leads to the hologram is an extension of this measuring tradition. Dennis Gabor was interested in better optical images of atomic structures than could be obtained with the microscopes of the late 40s. The earliest images of such structures had been produced by Sir Lawrence Bragg in 1929. These led him to the creation of the x-ray microscope, the device Gabor thought to improve, essentially by using a coherent light source – that is a light source in which, unlike, say, natural light, the waves are in phase with each other. Using a high-pressure mercury lamp he was able to produce a miniature photograph of an object's diffraction pattern. It had to be small because the method required that the object 'knocks a hole' (or 'wave front') in the larger beam coming from the source. 'Most of the waves would continue undisturbed but there would be an object-shaped "hole" where the object blocked part of the incident wavefront.'[8] A photographic plate registered the difference between the light source waves and the interference caused to them by the object. This was the first hologram – a true three-dimensional illusion which altered its appearance as the eye moved around it just as it would do in reality.[9]

The interference hypothesis Gabor exploited in 1947 had been known for nearly 150 years. Thomas Young, the 'universal genius'[10] who proposed the three-colour receptor concept discussed in Chapter Two above, also made this major contribution to the wave theory of light. In 1801 he was conducting an experiment using a coherent monochromatic light source, sodium, which he passed through a narrow slit. When he opened a second slit lit by the same source, he noticed the area illuminated by the first slit darkened. He hypothesised that this was because light did indeed exist in waves[11] and that when the second slit opened, the crests of the light waves coming through the first slit were cancelled by the troughs of the waves passing through the second. One set of waves *interfered* with the other. He was able to use this to calculate, with some degree of accuracy, the different wavelengths of colour. Subsequently, it became possible to capture such information photographically as an interference pattern. This is what Gabriel Lippmann had done in order to create his dyeless colour photochromes of 1891, described in Chapter Two.

Gabor could go no further with his researches because he lacked a strong, stable, coherent light source. Devices to produce such a source began to emerge in the late 1950s, their theoretical basis having been established decades earlier. Niels Bohr had suggested in 1913 that atoms in a low-energy state could be excited into a higher-energy state by absorbing quanta of light, 'photons' as Einstein called them. The converse was also true: if the atom were excited by light of the correct wavelength then a stream of photons would be produced as it decayed into its low-energy, ground state. What prevented an avalanche of photons being produced was that the atom began to reabsorb them. By the 50s, work was underway to produce a technique where this 'population inversion' would not occur; where, in fact, the number of excited atoms in the substance was always greater than the number in the ground state. The supervening necessity for turning such a theoretical concern into a practical technique was quite clear. Electronic communications depended on amplification and amplification still largely depended, as it had done for the previous half-century, on comparatively unreliable triode tubes (valves). Many research programmes, including that at the Bell Labs which had produced the transistor, were directed at this problem. Emissions of the sort Bohr described could perhaps be made to amplify signals as well.

The first solutions, both in America and in the USSR, created avalanches of microwaves, that is, invisible emissions, in devices known as MASERs (Microwave Amplification by Simulated Emission of Radiation). In a paper written in 1958, Charles Townes and A. L. Schawlow suggested how this might also be done with visible waves and proposed potassium vapour as the substance. This was at the height of post-Sputnik Cold War hysteria in the US and there was a particular need to produce systems that would allow for electronic communications over long distances, transoceanically or celestially. The Townes and Schawlow proposal for Light Amplification by Simulated Emission of Radiation – LASER – could contribute to such a system.

Potassium, however, did not turn out to be the answer to the 'population inversion' problem. Nikolai Basov and Aleksandre Prokhorov of the Lebedev Institute (who together had produced a maser in 1954) and Theodore Mainman of Hughes Aircraft achieved a laser effect using rubies by 1960. Thereafter many lasers were demonstrated with different substances but it was the two Russians and Townes who shared the Nobel Prize for Physics in 1964 'for the construction of oscillators and amplifiers based on the maser–laser principle.'[12]

Unexpectedly, at least in terms of the research agenda which had produced it, the laser, as a coherent light source, turned out to be ideal for making holograms. In 1963 the first laser-based holograms were produced by Emmett Leith and Juris Upatnieks.[13] Their system splits the laser-beam, one part of which is deflected on to a mirror and thence on to the photographic plate. The other part passes across the object onto the plate which therefore records the interference pattern created by the object. No lens or shutter is involved and the developed plate contains no identifiable image. Placing a coherent light source (i.e. a laser) behind the plate produces a true three-dimensional image of the object in front of the plate. As you walk round the hologram, your parallax view of the object changes just as it would if the object were solid and actually before you (see figure overleaf).

At about the same time, Yuri Denisyuk was applying Lippmann's techniques to capture not colour wavelength information but spatial information in the form of an interference pattern. Denisyuk's images were designated Lippmann-Bragg, or reflection, holograms.[14]

The main initial application of both techniques was for measurement. A holographic interferometer will instantly reveal, for example, deviations between an original and its copies. These show up as fringes or disturbances around the edges of the object. This allows for non-destructive testing and

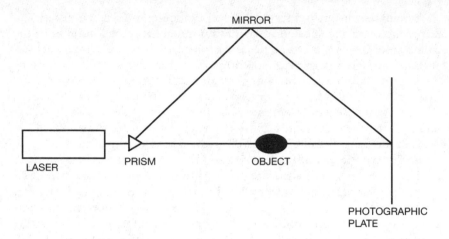

over the last thirty years has become a well-established and economic industrial technique.[15] There have been a number of significant advances. Holographic imaging has been used in integrated circuit design processes.[16] Colour was being explored from the very beginning when Leith and Upatnieks simply used three lasers trichromatically in a complex array. Denisyuk, already working with Lippmann's photochrome method, also used it to record the colour wavelengths in his reflection holograms.[17]

The way in which holography has been most widely diffused arises from an advance made in 1968 by Stephen Benton, then at the Polaroid lab, where he demonstrated, following Denisyuk, a rainbow hologram that did not require a laser for playback. RCA produced a system for embossing such images on plastic but it was not until a decade later, in a 1982 promotional campaign in connection with *E. T.* for the candy Reece's Pieces, that it was put to popular and widespread use. Two million packages with a holographic sticker caught the eye of the chief executive of American Bank Note Inc. He then sold the idea of embossed holograms to the credit card companies as a security measure or, since Benton himself has gone on record as not being convinced holograms actually make the cards more secure, then certainly as a marketing device. Holographic printing was also becoming more of a commonplace. For example, a hologram of an American eagle on the cover of the March 1984 edition of *National Geographic* demonstrated that millions of holograms could be produced in this way.[18]

Given that interferometry is not widely known, it is scarcely surprising that holography means little more to most people than these sorts of gimmicks. Nevertheless, its industrial and scientific potential has meant that steady, albeit unsensational, progress is being made. For example, much work has been done to make the images ever larger. Benton himself went on to the Media Lab at MIT and spent the 80s working on holograms big enough to speed up automotive design processes. Instead of elaborate, hand-crafted clay mock-ups, a computer-aided design (CAD) hologram could serve as well, being more quickly and easily altered as well as more cost-effective to produce. Benton's work at MIT was supported by General Motors.

114

Where does all this fit into our model? Holography figures as a series of further factors in the ground of scientific competence (the interference hypothesis, the creation of the laser), with the emergence of the hologram and the techniques of holographic interferometers and white-light holograms as true, if very early, prototypes of our holographic moving image system. Scientific and industrial imaging requirements constitute the supervening social necessity for these developments.

Holography as a 'Time-Based Medium'

When it comes to the holographic moving image, we are in the realm of phylogeny: for the last quarter of a century, holography has been recuperating the entire history of photography and cinematography. Holography, like photography, has been positioned as a still medium of which the 'primary visual property is that of producing "illusionistic" three-dimensional pictures – a kind of spatial photograph, with an added dimension'.[19] Yet, as with photography and cinematography, there is an easy blurring between stopping motion and creating it – at least in theory. Certainly, interferometry often involves stopping motion to produce holograms of real-time phenomenon such as speeding bullets or metals under stress.[20] Moving from these to sequences of holographic images is, however, difficult. Instead of the conceptual confusions of Muybridge and Marey, with holography there are a number of actual technical problems.

First of all, the continuous lasers used for the earliest holograms do not register objects that vibrate more than a fraction of the wavelength of light. Instead, a sort of black 3-D negative hole appears in the holographic image. Even the stillness of the earliest daguerreotype sitter would not be enough to stop the vibrations and allow the image to register. The solution is to use a pulsed laser with a short enough burst, a matter of nanoseconds, to avoid the vibration. Initially it was suggested that such minimal exposure time would require the laser to be so powerful as to run the danger of damaging the subject's eyes but in the event this proved not to be the case. A moving holographic image of fish in an aquarium was produced in 1969. The result could be seen by one person at a time. The holographic movie had reached, both in terms of its audience size and duration, the Kinetoscope stage.[21] There it was to stay. Holograms do not easily enlarge and the size of the image is dictated by the size of the recording medium. To make an image say 2m × 8m would require a film of that size. Handling and projecting such a film would be difficult but images of a cow and a living-room have been made in Sweden and Australia.

Television is no easier. Conventional signals are simply inadequate to carry the amount of information a holographic image would require nor can holograms be scanned. Nevertheless, with sufficient bandwidth, the interference information ought to be encodable and transmittable with the holograph being formed on the face of the tube and projected out into the space directly in front of it.

The problem in essence is that no widespread supervening necessity requires that these difficulties be overcome. The exploration of moving holograms has been left to a few artists who were initially interested in the technique as a new sort of photographic medium. Scattered all over the world, only a few institutions, such as the Museum of Holography founded in New York in 1986, have given them any sustained focus. The result is that an intermittent stream of short time-based holographic images ('holo-cinema'?; 'holomovies'?[22]) have appeared.

The first technique this disparate group of researchers, painters, sculptors, photographers/film-makers and video artists utilised was the capacity of the hologram, which has yet to be otherwise exploited, to store multiple two-dimensional images. (At the outset there was talk of whole books on one holographic plate, for example.) Lloyd Cross made integral or multiplex holograms of a series of two-dimensional cine-frames, the most famous being *Kiss II* (1974), of a woman winking and blowing a kiss. It was made of 540 frames and could be viewed in ordinary light.[23] (Although this could be seen by more than one person at a time, the echoes of the Kinetoscope remain strong. The first cries for film censorship were occasioned by an Edison film, originally shot for the Kinetoscope in 1896, entitled *The Kiss*.)

The sculptor Alexander took this technique a stage further in his eight-minute piece *The Dream* (1987) This consists of a series of integral holograms mechanically transported before the playback light source and viewed through a small window. Such quasi-Wheel-of-Life systems are also being explored in Japan at the Nippon Telephone Company lab.

Another approach was to use sequences of holographic 3-D images rather than multiplexes. In the 80s, two workers at the Experimental Cinema Laboratory of the University of Paris, Claudine Eizykman and Guy Fihman, produced a whole series of 35mm and 70mm mini-films with this technique. In 1985 they unveiled *Un nu*, a five-minute piece on 126mm in which a young woman done up as a mummy unbandages herself. The film could be seen by only one person at a time in a structure seven feet high, two feet wide and twenty-eight inches deep. At the same time, researchers at the Franco-German Defence Research Establishment produced a series of movies using reflection holography on 35mm and 126mm including, with the aid of Alexander, a version of *Beauty and the Beast* (1986) which lasts for eighty seconds.

All these pioneers are the Mareys, Muybridges and Edisons – if not the Friese-Greenes – of the holographic cinema. The nearest we have yet come to Lumière is Victor Komar who demonstrated a forty-seven-second movie on a holographic screen big enough for four people to view in 1976. By 1984 he had produced a five-minute holographic colour movie. By 1990 he was reportedly without funds to continue his work. By 1995 he had reportedly retired.

It is possible that we will never have a holographic movie system based on the model of the cinema. It is more likely that the application of computing power to holographic image-making will produce a televised medium with digitalisation solving the bandwidth and other problems. But what is quite clear at this time is that no supervening social necessity is accelerating such a development. What we have is a species of stasis where such necessities as exist – for industrial or military applications – are explored, as with the General Motors programme at the Media Lab, while further applications are not. The accelerator is stuck and these necessities are balanced by the constraints of other commercially determined research agenda as well as apparently more readily available 3-D technologies – virtual reality techniques, for example.

The agenda for refining existing television, outlined in the last chapter, is probably the most potent of these suppressive forces. We are currently in the early stages of a change to high-definition digital television. This will take, indeed has already taken, some decades. New display technologies (flat screens) are also being heavily developed and will obviously mesh with digital HDTV. Not until all this is diffused, a matter for more than one decade, will an industrial and commercial window open for holographic television.

By that time, the real limitation of the current virtual reality research agenda will also have become apparent. For example, placing video screens so close to the eyes, as the VR helmet requires, is almost certainly far from being a healthy idea as more than a quarter of a century's negative experience with radio emissions from display terminals suggests. I do not expect that this alone will halt current developments, any more than the same species of hazard has impacted on the diffusion of the mobile phone, but in this era of carcinogenic scares a pause is not inconceivable. Such a moment would again open a window for holographic movie systems.

The point is that the general addiction to realism is not powerful enough to overcome these constraints, upset the balance or depress the accelerator. Half a century after Gabor, the model looks like this:

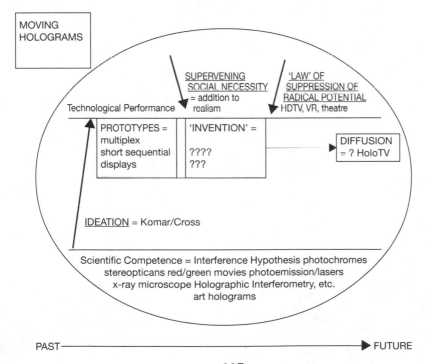

117

Only one thing is certain: if and when a holographic moving-image system is diffused, all this will be forgotten. Amnesiac about our technological history, befuddled by technological determinism, we will greet the arrival of HoloTV as the inevitable result of the unstoppable and ever speedier progress of science and technology. The fact that it will have taken decades, if not a century, to be diffused will go unremarked. And it might never happen!

Borges imagines an heresiarch of the land of Tlön who believes: 'Copulation and mirrors are abominable. ... the visible universe was an illusion or (more precisely) a sophism. Mirrors and fatherhood are abominable because they multiply and disseminate that universe.'[24] Perhaps HoloTV will be abominable too and never diffused. After all, we are here approaching the ultimate illusion – a true three-dimensional system of representation at the limits of human visual acuity. The image will be as real as the experience of the theatre – and perhaps for that reason alone will be redundant and never exploited.

The technologies of seeing bring us ever closer to a sort of Borgesian map of reality – one that corresponds at all points with the external world – but as they do so, they do little to help us understand their own historical and social realities. On the contrary, their basic illusionism disguises their artifice, their cultural formation and their ideological import. These essays have been attempts to penetrate the disguise.

Notes

Introduction: Necessities and Constraints

1. Fernand Braudel, *Civilisation and Capitalism, 15th–18th Century. Volume 1. The Structures of Everyday Life: The Limits of the Possible* (New York: Harper Row, 1979), p. 430.
2. Raymond Williams, *Television: Technology and Cultural Form* (London: Fontana, 1974), p. 13.
3. Quoted in the *Guardian*, 1 May 1995.
4. Mo Mowlam, 'Paper Tigers', *New Statesman & Society* vol. 7 no. 319/vol. 90 no. 1642, 9 September 1995, p. 24.
5. Raymond Williams, *The Politics of Modernism* (New York: Verso, 1989), p. 120.
6. This easy insult is itself an expression of technological determinism and concomitant historical ignorance in that it betrays a serious misunderstanding of the Luddites' actual campaign which was less to do with machines than with terms of trade. See E. P. Thompson, *The Making of the English Working Class* (Harmondsworth: Penguin, 1968), p. 600.
7. I am conscious of hearing Guy Cumberbatch use this image in connection with those who believe it is violent media material which causes violence in society. It seems to me to fit just as well here.
8. Braudel, *Civilisation and Capitalism. Volume 1*, p. 431.
9. Fernand Braudel, *Civilisation and Capitalism, 15th–18th Century. Volume 3. The Perspective of the World* (New York: Harper Row, 1979), p. 567.
10. Simon Lavington, *Early British Computers* (Manchester: Manchester University Press, 1980), pp. 16–22.
11. Brian Winston, *Misunderstanding Media* (London: Routledge & Kegan Paul; Cambridge, Mass.: Harvard University Press, 1986), pp. 159–60. (A revised version is in press.)
12. Ibid., pp. 315–37.
13. Ibid., passim.

Chapter 1: The Case of the Cinema

1. Josef Maria Eder, *History of Photography*, trans. Edward Epstean (New York: Dover, 1978), pp. 422–4.
2. Ibid., p. 489.
3. Ibid., pp. 485–6.
4. Ibid., p. 38.
5. William Irvins, Jr., *On the Rationalization of Sight* (New York: Da Capo, 1973), p. 16.

6. Robert Temple, *The Genius of China: Three Hundred Years of Science, Discovery and Invention* (New York: Simon and Schuster, 1986), pp. 87–8.
7. H. Mark Gosser, 'Kircher and the Lanterna Magica: A Re-examination', *SMPTE Journal*, October 1981, pp. 972–5; Eder, *History of Photography*, p. 52.
8. Horner is one of many who developed the basic idea of the 'Wheel of Life'. He was English (British?). It is hard to know why he has been singled out here.
9. 'What is generally recalled of the Lumière brothers' discovery is that it allowed for the representation of the moving image. Other endeavours had preceded it although without achieving the same success, from Horner's zootrope (1834) to Dickson and Edison's kinetoscope (1891) via Muybridge's experiments with the zoopraxiscope (1877) and Marey's 'photographic gun' (1881). On the technical level, however, Louis and Auguste Lumière were in 1895 the first to achieve the meeting of the kinetoscope and the magic lantern. ... one needs to go a few years further back, to 1830, to the physiological explanation provided by Joseph Plateau relating to persistence of vision. Plateau's discovery was to herald the cinema.' René Monnier, 'Le Protocole spectatoriel', *Interfaces: Image Texte Langue* no. 6, 1994, pp. 191–2.
10. Michael Chanan, *The Dream That Kicks: The Prehistory and Early Years of the Cinema in Britain* (London: Routledge and Kegan Paul, 1980), pp. 61–4.
11. R. L. Gregory, *Eye and Brain* (London: Weidenfeld and Nicolson, 1966), pp. 109–11; Bill Nichols and Susan Lederman, 'Flicker and Motion in Film', in Teresa de Laurentis and Stephen Heath (eds), *The Cinematic Apparatus* (New York: St Martin's Press, 1980), pp. 96–103. See also, for an account of the 'outstanding theoretical issues concerning apparent motion', Stephen Grossberg, 'Neural Facades: Visual Representations of Static and Moving Form-and-Colour-and-Depth', in Glyn Humphreys (ed.), *Understanding Vision* (Oxford: Blackwell, 1992), pp. 256–71.
12. Chanan, *The Dream That Kicks*, p. 55.
13. André Bazin, *What Is the Cinema? Volume One* (Berkeley: University of California Press, 1967), p. 19.
14. Chanan, *The Dream That Kicks*, p. 71.
15. Arthur Booth, *William Harvey Fox-Talbot: Father of Photography* (London: Arthur Barker, 1965), p. 196. I am grateful to Peter Twaites for this reference.
16. Eder, *History of Photography*, p. 346.
17. Janet Staiger, 'Combination and Litigation: Structures of US Film Distribution, 1896–1917', in Thomas Elsaesser (ed.), *Early Cinema: Space, Frame, Narrative* (London: BFI, 1990), p.189.
18. Eder, *The History of Photography*, pp. 492–4.
19. Ibid., pp. 506–7.
20. Gordon Hendricks, *The Edison Motion Picture Myth* (Berkeley: University of California Press, 1961), *passim*.
21. Dickson himself also does something of this. His account of the development of the Kinetoscope mentions Edison only to point out that he went abroad 'in the midst of the work'. Dickson begins a memoir by explaining how he wrote to Edison from London asking for a place but received a very negative answer. Nevertheless, he left for the New World with his mother and sisters and, after a two-year sojourn in Richmond, Virginia, at age 21 he presented himself to the great man. '"But I told you not to come", said Mr. Edison. I agreed but told him I couldn't have done otherwise after reading about the work in which he was engaged. ... He only replied, " ... you had better take

your coat off and get to work." I had won.' (W. K. Laurie Dickson, 'A Brief History of the Kinetograph, the Kinetoscope and the Kino-phonograph', *Journal of the SMPE* vol. 21, December 1933, reprinted in Raymond Fielding (ed.), *A Technological History of Motion Pictures and Television* (Berkeley: University of California Press, 1967), pp. 9–16).

22. See, for example, Harold Bowen , 'Thomas Alva Edison's Early Motion-Picture Experiments', *Journal of the SMPE* vol. 64, September 1955, reprinted in Raymond Fielding (ed.), *A Technological History of Motion Pictures and Television* (Berkeley: University of California Press, 1967), pp. 90–96.

23. W. H. G. Armytage, *A Social History of Engineering* (Boulder: Westview Press, 1976), p. 110.

24. Robert Friedel and Paul Israel, with Bernard Finn, *Edison's Electric Light: Biography of an Invention* (New Brunswick: Rutgers University Press, 1986), pp. 224–8.

25. Chanan, *The Dream That Kicks*, pp. 87–93.

26. Hendricks, *The Edison Motion Picture Myth*, pp. 11–12.

27. Staiger, 'Combination and Litigation', p. 190.

28. Louis Lumière, 'The Lumière Cinematograph', *Journal of the SMPE* vol. 27, December 1936, reprinted in Raymond Fielding (ed.), *A Technological History*, p. 36.

29. Charles Musser, *The Emergence of Cinema* (New York: Charles Scribner's Sons, 1990), p. 111.

30. Ibid., pp. 145-57, 170-79.

31. Bowen, 'Thomas Alva Edison', p. 94.

32. George Eastman, letter to F. H. Richardson, *SMPTE Journal* vol. 85, July 1976, p. 586; reprinted from *The Journal of the SMPE*, September 1925, p. 64.

33. Bowen, 'Thomas Alva Edison', p. 90.

34. Hendricks, *The Great Edison Movie Myth*, p. 63.

35. Thomas Edison, letter to F. H. Richardson, *SMPTE Journal* vol. 85, July 1976, p. 574, reprinted from *The Journal of the SMPE*, September 1925, p. 64.

36. Terry Ramsaye, *A Million and One Nights* (New York: Simon and Schuster, 1926), p. 63.

37. James Card, 'The Historical Motion-Picture Collections at George Eastman House', *Journal of the SMPTE* vol. 68, March 1959, reprinted in Raymond Fielding (ed.), *A Technological History*, pp. 106–7.

38. Staiger, 'Combination and Litigation', pp. 190–91.

39. Richard Barsam, *The Vision of Robert Flaherty: The Artist as Myth and Filmmaker* (Bloomington: Indiana University Press, 1988), p. 15.

40. Musser, *The Emergence of Cinema*, p. 345.

41. In 1929, 70mm reappeared unsuccessfully as Natural Vision or Grandeur and then, more effectively, in the 50s in the form of Panavision 70. James Limbacher, *Four Aspects of the Film* (New York: Brussel & Brussel, 1968), p. 132.

42. Staiger, 'Combination and Litigation', pp. 194–6.

43. Ibid., p.197.

44. Ibid., pp. 198–205. She also points out that the received story of Hollywood being established by independent producers fleeing the Trust is unfounded since it was licensed film-makers who were the first to reach Los Angeles and, anyway, the trade press carried full information on production so there really was nowhere to hide.

45. This is the technique of Josef Maria Eder, whose *Geschichte der Photographie*, the fourth edition (1932) of which was translated by Edward Epstean, is a

major source book for the great man approach. It runs to 860 pages in the American paperback edition of 1978. Despite this, even when discussing 'Daguerreotypy as a Profession, 1840-1860', he manages to say nothing about the social circumstances of the photographers he names – although he does mention, coyly, the earliest nudes and 'pictures of two persons which could not be reproduced' (p. 315). It takes Eder 193 pages to get to Niépce. He starts (to cite his chapter headings) 'From Aristotle (Fourth Century BC) to the Alchemists' and goes on to deal with such topics as 'Photochemical Research in the Eighteenth Century until Beccarius and Bonzius (1757)', 'Reflectography (Breyerotypy) by Albecht Breyer, 1839 ', 'Pigment Image by Contact: Marion (1873); Manly's Ozotype (1898); Ozobrome Process (1905); Carbo Prints' before he gets to his ninety-seventh and final chapter. It is only fitting that this edition concludes with an eight-page 'Biography of Josef Maria Eder by Hinricus Lüppo-Cramer'.

46. This is central to many of the other works I have been citing in this chapter, notably Musser, Chanan and the collection of essays edited by Thomas Elsaesser. In addition, one can note the pioneering 1971/72 essay of Jean-Louis Commoli using this approach ("Technique et Idéologie", *Cahiers du Cinéma* no. 229, pp. 4–21; no. 230, pp. 51-7; no. 231, pp. 39–45; nos. 234/35, pp. 94–100; no. 241, pp. 20–24). This new historiography of moving-image technology has not only influenced scholarship but penetrated deeply enough to begin to condition popular accounts of the origins of cinema in time for the Lumière centenary. A notable example of this was the BBC centenary series, *The Last Machine* (produced by John Wyver for Illuminations, directed by Richard Curson Smith, written by Ian Christie, presented by Terry Gilliam and transmitted in January 1995). Christie's book of the series, *The Last Machine: Early Cinema and the Birth of the Modern World* (London: BBC/BFI, 1994), has a somewhat more traditional feel in that it is punctuated by twenty-five 'great men' biographies, although it must be said three of these are of women and the rest embrace Russian, Polish, German and Italian pioneers as well as the usual parade of French, British and Americans.

47. A. D. Coleman, 'Lentil Soup', *Etc*, Spring 1985, p. 19.

48. G. Ten Doesschate, *Perspective: Fundamentals, Controversials, History* (Nieuwkoop: B. De graf, 1964), p. 85.

49. Svetlana Alpers, *The Art of Describing: Dutch Art in the Seventeenth Century* (Chicago: University of Chicago Press, 1984), pp. 53–64.

50. Joan Gadol, *Leon Battista Alberti: Universal Man of the Early Renaissance* (Chicago: University of Chicago Press, 1969), p. 25.

51. This has sometimes been seen as an essentially bourgeois mode of seeing but it is, at best, somewhat ahistorical to use such a term given that we are here some centuries before anything that could be called a bourgeois hegemony.

52. Peter Murray and Lynda Murray, *A Dictionary of Art and Artists* (Harmondsworth: Penguin Books, 1959), p. 265.

53. Lynda Nochlin, *Realism* (Harmondsworth: Penguin Books, 1971), p. 13.

54. Aaron Scharf, *Art and Photography* (Harmondsworth: Penguin Books, 1974), pp. 47–57.

55. Gisele Freund, *Photography and Society* (Boston: David R. Godine, 1982), p. 81.

56. Glynne Wickham, *A History of Theatre* (Oxford: Phaidon),1985, pp. 155, 181.

57. Ibid., p. 182.

58. John Fell, *Film and the Narrative Tradition* (Berkeley: University of California Press, 1974), pp. 137, 141; Chanan, *The Dream That Kicks*, pp. 112–44. This

tradition, fully narrativised, is now to be found in the very latest 'virtual reality' Disneyland and Universal tour rides where an audience, seated in chairs that bounce and tilt, is placed close-up to a large screen and undergoes the illusion of a violent travel narrative.

59. Ibid., p. 114.
60. Jean-Louis Comolli, 'Machines of the Visible', in Teresa de Laurentis and Stephen Heath (eds), *The Cinematic Apparatus* (New York: St Martin's Press, 1980), p. 122.
61. Musser, *The Emergence of Cinema*, pp. 22–27.
62. John Fell, *Film and The Narrative Tradition*, p. 140.
63. Ibid., pp. 15, 16.
64. Ibid., p. 139.
65. See a special edition on narrative of the *Journal of Communications* vol. 35 no. 4, Autumn 1985.
66. Seymour Chatman, *Coming to Terms: The Rhetoric of Narrative in Fiction and Film* (Ithaca: Cornell University Press, 1990), pp. 7, 9.
67. Gosser, 'Kircher and the Lanterna Magica ...', p. 974; Eder, *History of Photography*, p. 51.
68. I am not therefore persuaded by Tom Gunning's argument that there was an alternative to the narrative cinema, which he terms a 'cinema of attractions' in the first decade after 1895 and that narrative triumphed only after 1906/7. Gunning describes the cinema of attractions as 'less a way of telling stories than as a way of presenting a series of views to the audience' (Tom Gunning, 'The Cinema of Attractions: Early Film, Its Spectator and the Avant-Garde', in Thomas Elsaesser, ed., *Early Cinema: Space, Frame, Narrative*, London: BFI, 1990, p. 57). He suggests that 'the early cinema was not dominated by the narrative impulse that later asserted its sway over the medium' (ibid., p. 55); that is to say, cinema did indeed take a narrative 'turn'. He points to the dominance of actuality films, which outnumbered fiction until 1906; to the direct look of subjects at the lens; to the bowing and gesturing of variety artists again to the lens; to 'plotless trick films'; and to erotic exhibitionism as in *The Bride Retires*, a 1902 striptease film which, in Gunning's description, has the 'bride' winking at the camera while 'husband' peers at her from behind a screen. But much of his argument can be discounted; although, clearly, in so far as vaudeville acts were transferred to the screen, they remained non-narrative spectacles – i.e. with temporal structure but without (much) logical causality. In the first place most of these scenes unfold according to the double temporality which is, at the very least, a clue to the presence of narrative. Secondly, much of what Gunning suggests as having to do with display is sanctioned by theatrical practice. The 'bride' undresses – a simple narrative which is not altered by her awareness of the audience. Awareness of the audience is time-honoured in the theatre as is bowing to indicate closure, either of a trick or of a whole variety act.

A further basic problem here is an implicit claim for documentary difference, with the documentary being seen as essentially (and automatically) non-narrative. I have argued against this in *Claiming the Real* (London: BFI, 1995), pp. 99-123. Here let me just say that there might not be much of a narrative going on in the Lumières' 1895 film of *Workers Leaving the Factory* (*La Sorte des usines Lumière*) but the factory gates do open, a dog suddenly emerges – itself a somewhat curious mini-event – and the people move away and the gates close. There is no way this, and many other of these first fragments of time and space, can be typed except as simple narratives. They differ from the fictional films (if indeed such things as the presence of the dog does not give the lie even to this) simply because they are narrativised segments caught *sur le vif* rather than overtly set-up. Others argue that these 'documentary' films, *La Sorte des usines Lumière* and *L'Arrivée d'un train en gare de la Ciotat*, 'even if ... narratives, their level of narrativity bears no comparison to that of *L'Arroseur arrosé*' (André Gaudreault, 'Film, Narrative, Narration: *The Cinema of the Lumière Brothers*, in Thomas Elsaesser, ed., *Early Cinema: Space, Frame, Narrative* London: BFI, 1990, p. 69). But if narrative is defined in Chatman's terms, this notion of level refers to the strength of the causality within the narrative. It does not deny narrative's presence. In *L'Arroseur arrosé*, for example, A (the boy stepping on the hose) causes B (the gardener inspecting the suddenly inoperable hose) which causes C (the boy removing his foot) which causes D (the gardener getting soaked). In *La Sorte des usines Lumière*, the gates open (A) 'causing' the workers to exit (B) so that the gates can be shut (C). This may not be so engaging but it is still a narrative (as is Méliès's blowing up the magician's head, bigger and bigger and bigger and ... pouf). As Gunning points out, escaping from the prison house of narrative is an avant-garde project. It was as avant-garde an ambition before 1906 as it was to be afterwards.

Let me just add that I am not using the term 'simple' in any pejorative sense. It is wrong to see early deviations from later practices as primitive; rather such deviations can be noted, in Kristin Thompson's phrase, as 'a system apart'. This system differed not by being non-narrative but only by assuming the audience was in a theatrical situation i.e. locked into a seat and having therefore a fixed point of view (David Bordwell, Janet Staiger and Kirsten Thompson, *The Classical Hollywood Cinema: Film Style and Mode of Production to 1960* New York: Columbia University Press, 1985, p. 158). This is an alternative to the dominant mode, which came to utilise changes of viewpoint, ellipsis, etc., just as Soviet practice in the 20s or certain avant-garde procedures are also alternatives to the dominant mode. But unlike the avant-garde (but like the Soviets), the early fixed-viewpoint single-shot films are an alternative *narrative* mode. Cinema is not a question of *langue ou language* but rather *langues ou languages*.

69. Stephen Bottomore, 'Shots in the Dark: The Real Origins of Film Editing', in Thomas Elsaesser (ed.), *Early Cinema: Space, Frame, Narrative* (London: BFI, 1990), p. 104.

70. Ibid., p. 105.

71. Ibid.

72. Eric Hobsbawm, *The Age of Revolution, 1789-1848* (London: Weidenfeld & Nicolson, 1995), pp. 169–70.

73. Jan de Vries, *European Urbanisation, 1500-1800*, quoted in Eric Hobsbawm, *The Age of Empire 1875-1914* (London: Weidenfeld & Nicolson 1995), p. 343.

74. Eric Hobsbawm, *The Age of Capital, 1848–1875* (London: Weidenfeld & Nicolson, 1995), p. 210.

75. Hobsbawm, *The Age of Empire*, p. 137.

76. Hobsbawm, *The Age of Capital*, p. 236.

77. James Curran and Jean Seaton, *Power without Responsibility* (London: Routledge, 1999) pp. 25–49.

78. Chanan, *The Dream That Kicks*, pp. 137–42, 147–54.

79. Raymond Williams, *Culture and Society* (New York: Columbia University Press, 1983), pp. 306, 307.

80. Claire Tomalin, *Mrs. Jordan's Profession: The Story of a Great Actress and a Future King* (Harmondsworth: Penguin, 1995), pp. 28–31.

81. Kathleen Barker 'Bristol at Play, 1801–53: A Typical Picture of the English Provinces?', in David Mayer and Kenneth Richards (eds), *Western Popular Theatre* (London: Methuen 1977), p. 91.
82. Wickham, *History of the Theatre*, pp. 209–10.
83. John Allen, *A History of the Theatre in Europe* (London: Heinemann, 1983), p. 275.
84. Chanan, *The Dream That Kicks*, pp. 159–60.
85. Ibid., p. 38.
86. Hobsbawm, *The Age of Capital*, p. 276.
87. Ibid., p. 285.
88. Ibid., p. 286.
89. Hobsbawm, *The Age of Empire*, p. 221.
90. Allen, *A History of the Theatre in Europe*, p. 245.
91. Robert Allen, *Vaudeville and Film, 1895-1915: A Study in Media Interaction* (New York: Arno Press, 1980), pp. 26–8, 36.
92. Ibid., p. 39.
93. Chanan, *The Dream That Kicks*, pp. 167–9.
94. Musser, *The Emergence of Cinema*, pp. 276, 277.
95. André Bazin, *What Is the Cinema?*, p. 19.
96. Hobsbawm, *The Age of Empire*, p. 238.
97. Michael Chanan, 'Economic Conditions of Early Cinema', in Thomas Elsaesser (ed.), *Early Cinema*, p. 175.
98. Bazin, *What Is the Cinema?*, p. 18.
99. Implied in this view appears to be a vision of the nineteenth-century engineer as a *bricoleur*, a bodger. '*Bricolage*' is defined as a knocking together of things at hand (Channan, *The Dream That Kicks*, p. 51). This is the suggested obverse of modern scientific and technological procedures. I have elsewhere argued that such a position tends to see nineteenth-century technology in a false light from two points of view (Winston, *Misunderstanding Media*, pp. 373–80). In the first place, those who produced the cinema were at the heart of structured technological activities – Edison with is team in his industrial lab and Lumière in his far from small photographic factory. It is perhaps worth remembering that the credit for the moving image rests with these men and their helpers, not with the other 'great men' – the lonely Friese-Greene, the somewhat flamboyant Muybridge nor even the scientific Marey. Secondly, it is by no means the case that we now proceed in these matters in a less serendipitous way than we did last century. Take, for example, the creation of the transistor, often cited as the locus classicus of modern structured innovation (*Misunderstanding Media*, pp. 185–94). But, on the contrary, so serendipitous was the achievement of transistor effect that the Bell Lab had to delay announcing it to the world until the research team could work out some coherent physical explanation for the phenomenon in order to secure the patent. It is certainly the case that limited research agendas, such as the one detailed in Chapter Four for analogue high-definition television, are very structured; but no more so than was the rapid search for a viable telephone after the patents were granted to Bell and Gray for systems which did not quite work (*Misunderstanding Media*, pp. 330–37).
100. Chanan, *The Dream That Kicks*, p. 53.
101. Ibid., p. 123.
102. Musser, *The Emergence of Cinema*, p. 19.
103. Eder, *History of Photography*, p. 421.
104. Ibid., p. 422.

105. Ibid., p. 500.
106. Ibid., p. 514. I should add that this pattern is not uncommon. Some examples: Francis Ronalds proposed (and indeed built) a static electric telegraph in 1816, twenty-one years before Morse, but was ignored. The principle of the telephone was enunciated in 1831, and in 1861 (seventeen years before Bell and Gray) Philip Reiss built a device that came close enough to working to be used in anti-Bell patent actions. And then there is D. E. Hughes (who is credited with the microphone) who demonstrated radio in 1879 (sixteen years before Marconi) but was told he had done no such thing and so abandoned his experiments (Winston, *Misunderstanding Media*, pp. 297–8, 307, 315–22, 245).
107. Allen, *Vaudeville and Film*, p. 146.
108. Ibid., p. 318.
109. Ibid., p. 87.
110. Musser, *The Emergence of Cinema*, p. 122.
111. William Uricchio and Roberta Pearson, *Reframing Culture* (Princeton: Princeton University Press, 1993), p. 27.
112. Douglas Gomery, *Shared Pleasures: A History of Movie Presentation in the United States* (Madison, WI: University of Wisconsin Press, 1912), pp. 8–13.
113. Allen, *Vaudeville and Film*, pp. 44–5.
114. Christie, *The Last Machine*, p. 7.
115. Allen, *Vaudeville and Film*, p. 103.
116. Musser, *The Emergence of Cinema*, p. 148.
117. Gomery, *Shared Pleasures*, p. 13.
118. Musser, *The Emergence of Cinema*, p. 276.
119. Allen, *Vaudeville and Film*, p. 227.

Chapter 2: The Case of Colour Film

1. Terry Eagleton, *Criticism and Ideology* (London: Verso, 1978), p. 20.
2. Roland Barthes, *Mythologies* (London: Paladin, 1973), p. 142.
3. John Berger, *Ways of Seeing* (London: BBC, 1972), p. 10.
4. Produced by the El Salvador Film and Video Project, directed by Diego de la Texera, El Salvador/Cuba 1981.
5. Johannes Kepler, quoted in Svetlana Alpers, *The Art of Describing: Dutch Art in the Seventeenth Century* (Chicago: Chicago University Press, 1984), p. 50.
6. A. D. Coleman, 'Lentil Soup', *Etc*, Spring 1985, p. 19.
7. It is commonly asserted that *Quattrocento perspectiva artificialis* (a.k.a. '*construzione legittima*') as theorised by Alberti is the ground upon which the *camera obscura portabilis*'s lens sits, but as Comolli (see n. 9) correctly points out, this dominance was not without exceptions. It seems rather that Albertian perspective is somewhat beside the point, and the apparatus, as refined by Kepler, replicates the effects of the major alternative Dutch system in that no Albertian 'window' is suggested between the artist and/or viewer, and the unified vanishing point, although capable of being accommodated to this system, was not as privileged as it was in Italy. See Alpers, *The Art of Describing*, pp. 53–7.
8. See Jean-Louis Baudry, 'Ideological Effects of the Basic Cinematographic Apparatus', trans. Alan Williams, *Film Quarterly* vol. 28 no.2, Winter 1974–5, pp. 39–47.
9. See Jean-Louis Comolli, 'Technique et idéologie: 1', *Cahier du Cinéma*, May/June 1971, pp. 4–21.

10. Peter Wollen, 'Cinema and Technology: A Historical Overview', in Teresa de Laurentis and Stephen Heath (eds), *The Cinematic Apparatus* (New York: St. Martin's Press, 1980), p. 24.

11. Eastman Kodak Co. press release CPl 8357NR, Rochester, New York, 25 January 1983, p.1; quoted in Coleman, 'Lentil Soup', p. 19.

12. Edward Branigan, 'Color and Cinema: Problems in the Writing of History', *Film Reader* no. 4, 1979, p. 22.

13. Roderick Ryan, 'Color in the Motion-Picture Industry', *Journal of the SMPTE* vol. 85, July 1976, p. 499.

14. Natalie Kalmus, 'Color Consciousness', *Journal of the SMPE* vol. 22, August 1935, pp. 139–140. The meeting was held by the Technicians Branch of the Academy of Motion Picture Arts and Sciences in Hollywood on 21 May 1935.

15. See, for example, Joseph Valentine, 'Make-Up and Set Painting Aid New Film', *American Cinematographer*, February 1939, p. 54.

16. R. W. G. Hunt, *The Reproduction of Colour* (London: John Wiley and Sons, 1967), p. 62.

17. Ibid., pp. 127, 157.

18. Kalmus, 'Colour Consciousness', p. 144.

19. Hunt, *Reproduction of Colour*, p. 26.

20. Eder, *History of Photography*, pp. 668–73.

21. The caveat is because all modern accounts in the photographic literature that consistently speak of the excellence of the Lippmann method also stress its limitations, but are written with no indication that modern materials have been used to duplicate the original experiments. Therefore, it is possible that the difficulties, originally highlighted by the inventors of other more diffused systems, have simply become part of the received history of photography and are, by now, more apparent than real.

22. E. J. Wall, *The History of Three-Color Photography* (Boston: American Photographic Publishing Company, 1925), p. 4.

23. Based on an understanding of three-colour printing systems which dated back to the 18th century, this neural model was outlined by the polymath Dr Thomas Young. He had described how the eye focuses as well as the nature of astigmatism, and in 1807 he published his theory of three types of neural receptor. (He also translated part of the Rosetta stone and, more pertinently in this context, demonstrated the wave theory of light. We will return to this in Chapter Five.) However, our knowledge of the physiology of colour perception remains limited – attested to, for instance, by the illogical colour constancy experiment, first demonstrated by Gaspard Monge in 1789 and still not satisfactorily explained. (Although some advances are being made, e.g. 'Why neon colours are sometimes perceived to spread across a scene' is explored by Stephen Grossberg, 'Neural Facades: Visual Representations of Static and Moving Form-and-Colour-and Depth', in Glyn Humphreys (ed.), *Understanding Vision* (Oxford: Blackwell, 1992), pp. 249.

24. Ryan, 'Color in the Motion Picture Industry', pp. 497–8.

25. Jay Leyda, *Kino* (New York: Collier Books, 1968), p. 47.

26. Ryan, 'Color in the Motion Picture Industry', p. 500. Additive processes persisted in television. In the NTSC system, three electron guns, like Maxwell's three filtered cameras, scanned the image by means of a system of mirrors. In the receiving cathode ray tube, clusters of red, blue and green phosphor dots – a system suggested in Germany by Fleschsig in 1938 but harking back to the Autochrome plate of the Lumière brothers marketed in 1907 – are activated to produce the original colours additively.

27. Eder, *History of Photography*, pp. 639–59.
28. Ibid., pp. 552–9; Wall, *History of Three-Color Photography*, p. 390.
29. Branigan, 'Colour and Cinema ... ', p. 24.
30. Dudley Andrews, 'The Post-War Struggle for Color', in Teresa De Laurentis and Stephen Heath (eds), *The Cinematic Apparatus* (New York: St. Martins Press, 1980), p. 69.
31. In 1955 Eastman Kodak revived the 16mm lenticular film because it could be developed faster than conventional subtractive colour stocks, and increasing the speed of development was suddenly of importance. Television prime-time colour programming was just starting and needed to be recorded for networking to the other coast. Kodak saw in lenticular colour film an opportunity to stunt the development of videotape recording, at this point just emerging from the experimental stage. Between September 1956 and February 1958 the pioneering network in colour, NBC, used Kodacolor film for making 'hot' (i.e., fast) kinescopes (or telerecordings); but in November 1956 CBS transmitted the first videotape programme. Sixteen months later NBC gave up and went to the videotape. There are no contemporary lenticular stocks.
32. Wall, *History of Three-Color Photography*, p. 406.
33. Ibid., p. 417.
34. Ibid., p. 158.
35. Ryan, 'Color in the Motion Picture Industry', p. 501.
36. Gorem Kindem, 'Hollywood's Conversion to Color: The Technological, Economic and Aesthetic Factors', *Journal of the University Film and Video Association* vol. 31 no. 2, Spring 1979, p. 34.
37. Ibid., p. 31.
38. Wesley Hanson, 'The Evolution of Motion Pictures in Color', *SMPTE Journal* vol. 89, July 1980, p. 501.
39. Peter Baxter, 'On the History and Ideology of Film Lighting', *Screen*, Autumn 1975, p. 92.
40. Ibid., p. 100.
41. Valentine, 'Make-Up ... ', p. 54. Photoelectric cells had been in production since 1911, and various light meters had been available but were considered as an unprofessional prop. It should be remembered that the norm in the studios at this time was to work constantly with one stop; therefore the lighting level remained constant from shot to shot and indeed from film to film.
42. Ed Buscombe, 'Sound and Colour', *Jump Cut*, April 1978, p. 25.
43. Ibid.
44. Dudley Andrew, 'The Post-War Struggle for Color', p. 72.
45. Ibid., p. 68.
46. Kalmus, 'Colour Consciousness', p. 141.
47. Steve Neale, *Cinema and Technology: Image Sound Colour*, London, BFI/Macmillan, 1985, p. 148.
48. David MacAdam, 'Quality of Color Reproduction', *Journal of the SMPTE* vol. 56, May 1951, pp. 487–518.

Chapter 3: The Case of 16mm Film

1. David Bordwell, Janet Staiger and Kirstin Thompson, *The Classical Hollywood Cinema* (New York, Columbia University Press, 1985), pp. 104–5.
2. 'Address by Henry D. Hubbard, Secretary, U.S. National Bureau of Standards, before the Society of Motion Picture Engineers, at its Washington Meeting,

Monday, July 24th, 1916', quoted in Gordon Chambers, 'A Short History of Standardisation in the SMPTE', *SMPTE Journal* vol. 85, July 1976, p. 454.

3. Joseph Maria Eder, *History of Photography*, trans. Edward Epstean (New York: Dover, 1978), p. 510; Charles Musser, *The Emergence of Cinema: The American Screen to 1907* (New York: Charles Scribners Sons, 1990), pp. 65–8.

4. Thomas Edison, 'Letter to Mr. Robertson, 24 January 1925'; reprinted in *SMPTE Journal* vol. 85, July 1976, p. 574.

5. Harold Bowen , 'Thomas Alva Edison's Early Motion-Picture Experiments', *Journal of the SMPE* vol. 64, September 1955, reprinted in Raymond Fielding (ed.), *A Technological History of Motion Pictures and Television* (Berkeley: University of California Press, 1967), pp. 95–6.

6. Musser, *The Emergence of Cinema*, p. 71.

7. Ibid., p. 72.

8. Eder, *History of Photography*, p. 509.

9. Glenn Matthews and Raife Tarkington, 'Early History of Motion Picture Film', *Journal of the SMPE* vol. 64, March 1955, reprinted in Fielding, *A Technological History ...* , pp. 129, 130.

10. Earl Theisen, 'The History of Nitrocellulose as a Film Base', *Journal of the SMPE* vol. 20, March 1933, reprinted in Fielding, *A Technological History ...*, p. 118.

11. Matthews and Tarkington, 'Early History ... ', p.130–32, fig. 3.

12. Ibid., pp. 130–31, Table 1.

13. Ibid., p. 137; Patricia Zimmermann, *Reel Families: A Social History of Amateur Film* (Bloomington: Indiana, 1995), p. 63.

14. Ibid., p.131.

15. Ibid., p.136.

16. Ibid., pp. 134–5.

17. See Patricia Zimmerman, *Reel Families, passim*.

18. Luke McKernan, *Topical Budget* (London: BFI, 1992), p. 4.

19. Ibid., pp. 3–8.

20. Richard Koszarski, *An Evening's Entertainment: The Age of the Silent Feature Picture, 1915-1928* (New York: Charles Scribner's Sons, 1990), p. 167.

21. Raymond Fielding, *The American Newsreel, 1911-1967* (Norman Oklahoma: University of Oklahoma Press, 1972), p. 228.

22. McKernan, *Topical Budget*, p. 7; Anthony Aldgate, *Cinema and History: British Newsreels and the Spanish Civil War* (London: Scolar, 1979), p. 37.

23. Ibid., pp. 35–7.

24. This is well documented in Aldgate and Fielding. See also Jonathan Lewis, 'Before Hindsight', *Sight and Sound* vol. 44 no. 2, Spring 1977, p. 46; Jeffrey Richards and Dorothy Sheridan, *Mass Observation at the Movies* (London: Routledge and Kegan Paul, 1987), *passim*; Brian Winston, 'The *CBS Evening News*, 7 April 1949: Creating an Ineffable Television Form', in J.E.T. Eldridge (ed.), *Getting the Message: News, Truth and Power* (London: Routledge, 1993), pp. 181-5.

25. Aldgate, *Cinema and History*, pp. 45–7.

26. Brian Winston, *Claiming the Real: The Documentary Tradition Revisited* (London: BFI, 1995), pp. 61–8.

27. John Grierson, 'Summary and Survey 1935', in Forsyth Hardy (ed.), *Grierson on Documentary* (London: Faber and Faber, 1979), p. 69.

28. Arts Council of Great Britain, *The Factual Film* (London: PEP/Geoffrey Cumberlege at the OUP, 1947), p. 21.

29. John Grierson, 'First Principles of Documentary', in *Grierson on Documentary*, p. 36.
30. Don Macpherson , 'Part V: Amateur Films – Introduction', *Traditions of Independence: British Cinema in the Thirties* (London: BFI, 1980), p. 196.
31. Kenneth Gordon, 'Cinema Log: Documentary Films Should Be the Professional's Province', *Cine-Technician* (London: ACT), May/June 1938, reprinted in Don Macpherson (ed.), *Traditions of Independence: British Cinema in the Thirties* (London: BFI, 1980), p. 206.
32. Macpherson, 'Part V: Amateur Films', p. 196.
33. Zimmermann, *Reel Families*, pp. 1–11.
34. World Film News, 'Police Use Cine-Camera to Convict Speedsters', May 1936, reprinted in Macpherson (ed.), *Traditions of Independence*, p. 125.
35. Eric Knight, 'No More Film Plays', in *Cinema Quarterly*, Autumn 1933, reprinted in Macpherson (ed.), *Traditions of Independence*, p. 202; Deke Dusinberre, 'The Avant-Garde Attitude in the Thirties', reprinted Macpherson (ed.), *Traditions of Independence*, p. 41; Victoria Wegg-Prosser, 'The Archive of the Film and Photo League', *Sight and Sound* vol. 46 no. 4, Autumn 1977, p. 246. Can it be an accident, given how few women were involved in the public activities of these film-makers, that these last two quotes are both from women – the first from Judith Todd writing in the first issue of *Film* and the second from Irene Nicolson writing in the first and last issue of *The Camera Forward*?
36. Bert Hogenkamp, 'Film and the Workers Movement in Britain', *Sight and Sound* vol. 43 no. 2, Spring 1976, p. 71.
37. Bert Hogenkamp, 'Workers Newsreels in Germany, the Netherlands and Japan during the Twenties and Thirties', in Thomas Waugh (ed.), '*Show Us Life*': *Toward a History and Aesthetics of Committed Documentary* (Metuchen, N.J.: The Scarecrow Press, 1986), pp. 53–55.
38. Bert Hogenkamp, *Deadly Parallels: Film and the Left in Britain, 1929-39* (London: Lawrence and Wishart, 1986), pp. 216–1.
39. Knight, 'No More Film Plays', p. 202.
40. Russell Campbell, 'Radical Cinema in the 1930s: The Film and Photo League', in Peter Stevens (ed.), *Jump Cut: Hollywood, Politics and Counter-Cinema* (Toronto: Between The Lines, 1985), p. 127.
41. Hogenkamp, *Deadly Parallels*, pp. 93–103.
42. Ralph Bond, 'This Montage Business', *Close-Up*, November 1929, reprinted in Macpherson (ed.), *Traditions of Independence*, p. 198.
43. Erik Chisholm, 'The Amateur Film Maker: Work or Play', *Cinema Quarterly* vol. 1 no. 1, Winter 1932/3, reprinted in Macpherson (ed.), *Traditions of Independence*, pp. 200–202.
44. Trevor Ryan, 'Film and Political Organisations in Britain, 1929-39', reprinted in Macpherson (ed.), *Traditions of Independence*, pp. 51–69.
45. Emilie De Brigard, 'The History of Ethnographic Film', in Paul Hockings (ed.), *Visual Anthropology* (The Hague: Mouton, 1975), p. 26.
46. David Macdougall, 'Prospects for the Ethnographic Film', *Film Quarterly* vol. 23 no. 2, Winter 1969/70, p. 29.
47. De Brigard, 'The History of the Ethnographic Film', p. 21; Winston, *Claiming the Real*, pp. 170-73.
48. Knight, 'No More Film Plays!', p. 202.
49. William Lafferty, 'The Blattnerphone: An Early Attempt to Introduce Magnetic Recording into the Film Industry', *Cinema Journal* vol. 22 no. 4, Summer 1983, pp. 18–37.

50. Michael Chanan, *Repeated Takes: A Short History of Recording and its Effect on Music* (London: Verso, 1995), pp 26–7.

51. Charles Musser, 'The Nickelodeon Era Begins: Establishing the Framework for Hollywood's Mode of Representation', in Thomas Elsaesser (ed.), *Early Cinema: Space Frame Narrative* (London: BFI, 1990), pp. 262–8.

52. Raymond Fielding, 'Antecedents', *Sound and the Cinema: The Coming of Sound to American Film*, ed. Evan William Cameron (Pleasantville, NY: Redgrave Press), pp. 6-23; William Greenwald, 'The Impact of Sound upon the Film Industry: A Case Study in Innovation', *Explorations in Entrepreneurial History* vol. 4 no. 4, May 15 1952, pp. 178-92.

53. Robert Allen and Douglas Gomery, *Film History: Theory and Practice* (New York: Knopf, 1985), p. 118.

54. G. R. M. Garratt and H. A. Mumford, 'The History of Television', *Proceedings of the Institution of Electrical and Electronic Engineers* vol. 99 part iii (A), 1952, reprinted in G. Shiers (ed.), *Technical Development of Television* (New York: The Arno Press, 1977), p. 26.

55. Raymond Fielding, 'Antecedents', p. 13.

56. Steve Neale, *Cinema and Technology: Image Sound Colour* (London: BFI, 1985), pp. 83–4.

57. Edward Kellogg, 'History of Sound Motion Pictures: First Installment', *Journal of the SMPTE* vol. 64, June 1955; Edward Kellogg, 'History of Sound Motion Pictures: Second Installment', *Journal of the SMPTE* vol. 64, July 1955; both reprinted in Raymond Fielding (ed.), *A Technological History of Motion Pictures and Television* (Berkeley: University of California Press, 1967), pp. 182–8; Fielding, 'Antecedents', pp. 15–21.

58. Douglas Gomery, 'Hollywood Converts', *Sound and the Cinema: The Coming of Sound to American Film*, ed. Evan Willaim Cameron (Pleasantville, NY: Redgrave Press), p. 27.

59. Greenwald, 'The Impact of Sound', pp. 179-180.

60. F. C. Waldrop and J. Borkin, *Television: A Struggle for Power* (New York: William Morrow, 1938), p. 128.

61. John Ehrenberg and Laurence Roberts, 'Seventy-Five Years of Motion Picture Standards: Contributions of the Bell & Howell Co.', *SMPTE Journal* vol. 92 no. 10, October 1983, p. 1062.

62. Knight, 'No More Film Plays!', p. 203.

63. Ibid.

64. Aaron Nmungwun, *Video Recording Technology* (Hillsdale, New Jersey: Lawrence Erlbaum, 1989), pp. 38–48.

65. Ibid., p. 49.

66. Lafferty, 'The Blattnerphone ... ', pp. 23–4; Nmungwun, *Video Recording Technology*, p. 55.

67. Ibid., pp. 58–64.

68. William Uricchio , 'Rituals of Reception, Patterns of Neglect: Nazi Television and its Postwar Representation', *Wide Angle* vol. 11 no. 1, 1989, pp. 48–66.

69. Douglas Gomery, 'Hollywood Converts to Sound: Chaos or Order?', in Evan William Cameron (ed.), *Sound and the Cinema: The Coming of Sound to American Film* (Pleasantville, NY: Redgrave Press, 1980), pp. 24-34.

70. Fielding, 'Antecedents', p. 21.

71. Nmungwun, *Video Recording Technology*, p. 78.

72. Hazard Reeves, 'The Development of Stereo Magnetic Recording for Film (Part 1)', *SMPTE Journal* vol. 91 October 1982, p. 950.

73. Lafferty, 'The Blattnerphone ... ', p. 20.
74. For a discussion on the power of the concept of amateurism see Zimmermann, *Real Families,* pp. 90-111.
75. Richard MacCann, *The People's Films: A Political History of US Government Motion Pictures* (New York: Hastings House 1973), p. 136.
76. H. D. Waley, 'British Documentaries and the War Effort, *Public Opinion Quarterly,* Winter 1942, p. 607, in Pronay and D. W. Spring (eds), *Propaganda, Politics and Film, 1918-45* (London: Macmillan, 1982); Helen Forman, 'The Non-Theatrical Distribution of Films by the Ministry of Information', in Pronay and Spring (eds), *Propaganda, Politics and Film,* p. 229.
77. Robert Allen and Douglas Gomery, *Film History: Theory & Practice* (New York: Knopf, 1985), p. 221.
78. Macpherson, 'Amateur Films: Introduction', p. 193.
79. Vincent Mosco, *Broadcasting in the United States: Innovative Challenge and Organizational Control* (Norwood, NJ.: Ablex, 1980), pp. 19–21.
80. Brian Winston, 'The *CBS Evening News,* 7 April 1949: Creating an Ineffable Television Form', in John Eldridge (ed.), *Getting the Message* (London: Routledge, 1993), pp. 203–205.
81. Anon., *Arri: 50 Years* (Munich: Arnold and Richter KG, n.d.), unpaged.
82. BKSTS, *Dictionary of Audio Visual Terms* (London: The Focal Press, 1983), p. 79.
83. Ehrenberg and Roberts, 'Seventy-Five Years of Motion-Picture Standards', *SMPTE Journal* vol. 92 no.10, October 1983, 1061-2 & illus. on p. 1063.
84. The advantages of the camera in this context were that it required very high levels of care and awareness to operate effectively. By the mid-80s, maintaining a supply of Filmos, around which the first production course was designed, was becoming a major problem.
85. Alvin Roe, '16mm Camera with Behind-the-Lens Meter', *American Cinematographer,* November 1964, pp. 644, 646.
86. Advertisement, 'Presenting Auricon Filmagnetic', *Journal of the SMPTE* vol. 64 December 1955, p. 705.
87. Walter Bach, E. M. Berndt, A. N. Brown and R. L. George, 'Magnetic 16mm Single-System Sound-on-Film-Recording Camera Equipment', *Journal of the SMPTE* vol. 65, November 1956, p. 603.
88. Ibid.
89. Ann-Ruth Martin, '16mm Magnetic Sound on TV Newsfilms in Germany, *Journal of the SMPTE* vol. 65, June 1956, pp. 336–7.
90. Edmund DiGiulio, 'Developments in Motion Picture Camera Design', *SMPTE Journal* vol. 85, July 1976, p. 485.
91. R. C. Rheineck, 'Striped Magnetic Sound in CBS Television News Production', *Journal of the SMPTE,* vol. 66, July 1957, p. 411.
92. Advertisement, 'Presenting Auricon Filmagnetic', p. 705.
93. DiGiulio, 'Developments in Motion Picture Camera Design', p. 486.
94. Bach et al., 'Magnetic 16mm Single-System ... ', p. 603.
95. Rheineck, 'Striped Magnetic Sound in CBS Television News Production', p. 412.
96. William Bluem, *Documentary in American Television* (New York: Hastings House, 1965), pp. 135, 137, 184.
97. Patricia Jaffe, 'Editing Cinéma Vérité', *Film Comment* vol. 3 no. 3, Summer 1965, p. 43.
98. Winston, *Claiming the Real,* pp. 145–163.

99. Anon., 'A New Lightweight Version of the Pro 600 ... ', *Journal of the SMPTE* vol. 69, September 1960, p. 701.

100. Mike Eaton (ed.), *Anthropology – Reality – Cinema: The Films of Jean Rouch* (London: BFI, 1970), pp. 2, 5.

101. Winston, *Claiming the Real*, pp. 181–8.

102. Jean Rouch, 'The Cinema of the Future?', *Studies in Visual Communication* vol. 11 no. 1, Winter 1985, p. 34 & stills on pp. 17, 18.

103. DiGiulio, 'Developments in Motion Picture Camera Design', p. 484.

104. Martin, '16mm Magnetic Sound on TV Newsfilms in Germany', p. 336.

105. William Stancil, 'A Self-Contained Recorder for Motion Picture Sound', *Journal of the SMPTE* vol. 70, August 1961, p. 597.

106. C. G. McProud, 'Tape Recorders, Tape and Equipment', *Audio*, February 1956, p. 34.

107. Albert Travis, 'Evolution of a Successful Spring-Driven, Broadcast-Quality Tape Recorder', *Journal of the Audio Engineering Society* vol. 7 no. 4, October 1959, p. 207.

108. McProud, 'Tape Recorders, Tape and Equipment', pp. 34, 36.

109. Albert Travis, 'Development of a Subminiature Tape Recorder', *Journal of the Audio Engineering Society* vol. 3 no. 2, April 1955, p. 91.

110. Anon., 'The Perfectone Model EP6A Portable Magnetic Recorder', *Journal of the SMPTE* vol. 68, March 1959, pp. 193–4.

111. Anon., 'The Perfectone EP6A Recorder and Ryder Sync Generators, Transformers ... ', *Journal of the SMPTE* vol. 70, June 1961, p. 472.

112. Loren Ryder, 'Improved Synchronizing System Using Magnetic Tape', *Journal of the SMPTE* vol. 70, June 1961, pp. 426–8.

113. DiGiulio, 'Developments in Motion Picture Camera Design', p. 485.

114. Ibid.

115. Anon., 'The Nagra III B', *Journal of the SMPTE* vol. 71, November 1962, p. 902.

116. Anon., 'Nagra Tape Recorder', *American Cinematographer*, December 1960, p. 762.

117. Rudolph Epstein and Leo O'Donnell, 'Tape Reproducing Equipment for Synchronization System', *Journal of the SMPTE* vol. 70, December 1961, pp. 972–5.

118. Hal Margargle, 'Let's Talk about Tape Synchronization', *Audio*, November 1962, pp. 25-6, 86-8.

119. Anon., 'Sennheiser MKH 104 Condenser Microphone', *Audio*, October 1963, p. 50.

120. Donald Anderson, Robert Winter and Reid Ray, 'A Method for Recording, Editing and Mixing Magnetic Sound for Industrial Films', *Journal of the SMPTE* vol. 68, May 1959, pp. 336–7.

121. Take British cinematographer 'Slim' Hewitt. On *Tonight*, the BBC nightly news magazine of the late 50s, he was the first to use 16mm because he was an outsider, a freelance without professional cinematographic experience. He was, in fact, a stillsman from the magazine *Picture Post*. When I worked with him in the mid-60s he was still using the EMI L2 with a blimped Arriflex. This had windows so you could see what the camera was doing, e.g. the footage counter. Slim's camera would sit on the tripod with the L2 placed on the spreader. He had built a series of mirrors into the windows of the blimp so he could sit eye to viewfinder, headphones on ears and monitor the whole rig without standing up. He saw no reason to invest in an Eclair.

Chapter 4: The Case of HDTV

1. Anon, 'Sony Does It Again in HDTV', *Broadcasting*, 4 May 1981, p. 29; Nicolas Mokhoff, 'A Step Toward "Perfect" Resolution', *IEEE SPECTRUM*, July 1981, p. 58.

2. Anon, 'Montreux: International Gathering of TV's Most Technical Minds', *Broadcasting*, 25 May 1981, p. 54; Anon, 'Meeting in Montreux: Focusing on the Future of Television', *Broadcasting*, 15 June 1981, pp. 68–9.

3. For example, Takashi Fujio, ' A Study of High-Definition TV System in the Future', *IEEE Transactions on Broadcasting*, vol. BC-24 no. 4, December 1978, p. 92. The identical phrase may be found in Takashi Fujio, Junichi Ishida, Taro Komoto and Taiji Nishizawa, 'High-Definition Television System – Signal Standard and Transmission', *SMPTE Journal* vol. 89, August 1980, p. 584.

4. Junichi Ishida, Taiji Nishizawa and Keiichi Kubota, 'High Definition Television Broadcasting by Satellite', *IEEE Transactions on Broadcasting* vol. BC-28 no. 4, December 1982, pp. 165–71.

5. C. P. Sandbank and M. E. B. Moffat, 'High Definition Television and Compatibility with Existing Standards', *SMPTE Journal* vol. 92, May 1983, p. 552.

6. Kenneth Donow and Marcia De Sonne, *HDTV: Planning for Action* (Washington: National Association of Broadcasters, 1988), p. 6.

7. Peter Goldmark and John Hollywood, 'A New Technique for Improving the Sharpness of Television Pictures', *Journal of the SMPTE* vol. 57, October 1951, p. 382.

8. P. Schagen, H. Bruining and J. C. Francken, 'The Image Iconoscope – A Camera Tube for Television', *Journal of the SMPTE* vol. 58, June 1952, p. 512.

9. Donald Fink, 'The Future of High-Definition Television: First Portion of a Report of the SMPTE Study Group on High-Definition Television', *SMPTE Journal* vol. 89, February 1980, p. 92.

10. Brian Winston, *Misunderstanding Media* (London: Routledge and Kegan Paul, 1986), p. 94. Although the Technicolor system never got off the ground, others were coming on stream by the late 70s.

11. Takashi Fujio et al., 'High-Definition Television System', p. 579.

12. Raymond Wilmotte, 'TV Look Ahead', *IEEE Spectrum*, February 1976, pp. 34-9; Raymond Wilmotte, 'Technical Frontiers of Television', *IEEE Transactions on Broadcasting* vol. BC-22 no. 3, September 1976, pp. 73 - 80. It can be noted that these tests are really rather crude averagings of subjectivities obtained, for example, by sitting 176 educational broadcasters in front on a screen on which the images were projected for 30 seconds. There have been attempts to make these procedures more sophisticated but the underlying subjective judgments are unavoidable. See, for example, C. A. Siocos, 'Numerical Values for Subjective Picture Quality in Television', *Journal of the SMPTE* vol.80, December 1971, pp. 958-62.

13. Kozo Hayabashi, 'Research and Development of High-Definition Television in Japan', *SMPTE Journal* vol 91, March 1982, p. 180.

14. Nora Lee, 'HDTV: The Artists Speak', *American Cinematographer*, September 1987, p. 86.

15. Wilmotte, 'Technical Frontiers of Television', pp. 78-80.

16. Wilmotte, 'TV Look Ahead', p. 37; Anon., 'Top of the Week', *Broadcasting*, 2 November 1981, p. 26.

17. Gary Arlen, Suzan Prince and Mark Trost, *Tomorrow's TV: A Review of New TV Set Technology, Related Video Equipment and Potential Market Impacts,*

1987–1995, Com/Tech Report Series (Washington: National Association of Broadcasters Research and Planning Department, January 1987), pp. 25-8.

18. Ronald Jurgen, 'Chasing Japan in the HDTV Race', *IEEE Spectrum*, October 1989, pp. 26-30.

19. R. N. Jackson and M. J. J. C. Annegarn, 'Compatible Systems for High-Quality Television', *SMPTE Journal* vol. 92 no. 7, July 1983, p.720.

20. Anon., 'HDTV through the 1980's: A Realization of the Broadcasters' Mandate', *HDTV Production Series no. 60*, Park Ridge, New Jersey, Sony Corporation of America, 4/88, p. 1.

21. Joseph Roizen, 'Dubrovnik Impasse Puts High-Definition TV on Hold', *IEEE Spectrum*, September 1986, p. 32.

22. Ibid.

23. Ibid., p. 33.

24. Jurgan, 'Chasing Japan', p. 26.

25. Mark Lywyn, 'USA Still Blurry on New Technology', *USA Today*, 18 November 1987, p. B2.

26. Frances Seghers et al., 'Television Makers Are Dreaming of a Wide Crispness', *Business Week*, 21 December 1987, p. 109.

27. William Marbach et al., 'Super Television', *Business Week*, 30 January 1989, p. 56.

28. Ibid.

29. Anon, 'Pentagon Help in TV Research', *The New York Times*, 19 December 1988, p. D5.

30. Calvin Sims, 'Sony Seeks TV Grant from US', *The New York Times* , 3 March 1989, p. D1.

31. David Sanger, 'Japanese Test Illustrates Big Lead in TV of Future', *The New York Times*, 21 March 1989, pp. A1/D10.

32. David Sanger, 'Few See Japan Make TV History', *The New York Times*, 26 November 1991, pp. D1/D10.

33. H. J. Schlafly, 'Some Comparative Factors of Picture Resolution in Television and Film Industries', *Journal of the SMPTE* vol. 56, January 1951, p. 50. Actually, in cinemas under test conditions, the projected 35mm image can be matched by a projected electronic image with a resolution somewhere between 700/800-lines. (See Arthur Kaiser, Henry Mahler and Renville McMann, 'Resolution Requirements for HDTV Based upon the Performance of 35mm Motion-Picture Films for Theatrical Viewing', *SMPTE Journal* vol. 94, June 1985, p. 656).

34. John Freeman, 'The Evolution of High-Definition Television', *SMPTE Journal* vol. 93, May 1984, pp. 492-501.

35. For example, Donald Fink, 'Color Television v. Color Motion Pictures', *Journal of the SMPTE* vol. 64, June 1955, p. 283, Table II.

36. Fink, 'The Future of High-Definition Television: First Portion ...', pp. 89-94; Donald Fink, 'The Future of High-Definition Television: Conclusion of a Report of the SMPTE Study Group on High-Definition Television', *SMPTE Journal* vol. 89, March 1980, pp. 153-61.

37. Ibid., p. 158.

38. Richard Stumpf, 'A Film Studio Looks at HDTV', *SMPTE Journal* vol. 94 March 1987, p. 251.

39. Ibid.

40. Anon, 'The Ever-Expanding Possibilities of Video', *Broadcasting*, 16 November 1981, p. 40.

135

41. Mike Bygrave and Joan Goodman, 'Meet Me in Las Vegas', *American Film*, October 1981, p. 43.
42. Susan Levin, 'High Definition Transfers to 35mm', *American Cinematographer*, May 1986, p. 86.
43. Louis Pourciau, 'High-Resolution TV for the Production of Motion Pictures', *SMPTE Journal* vol. 93, December 1984, p. 112.
44. Gary Arlen et al., *Tomorrow's TV*, p. 29.
45. Anon, 'Pioneering Rebo Studio Gives HDTV Uses in the Real World', *Variety*, 5 October 1988, p. 96.
46. Nora Lee, 'HDTV: The Artists Speak', pp. 85–87.
47. Anon, 'HDTV Provides Film-Broadcast Nexus at SMPTE', *Broadcasting*, 9 November 1987, p. 46.
48. Donow and De Sonne, *HDTV: Planning for Action*, pp. 11, 18.
49. Anon, 'Tech Bits', *Advanced Television Markets*, December/January 1992, p. 22.
50. Anon, 'Conclusion', *HDTV Production Series* no. 30, Park Ridge, New Jersey, Sony Corporation of America, April 1988, p. 8.
51. Harry Mathias, 'Image Quality from a Non-Engineering Viewpoint', *SMPTE Journal* vol. 93 no.8, August 1984, p. 712.
52. Ibid.
53. James Limbacher, *Four Aspects of the Film* (New York: Brussel & Brussel, 1968), pp. 107-16; John Belton, '1950s Magnetic Sound: The Frozen Revolution', in Rick Altman (ed.), *Sound Theory Sound Practice* (London: Routledge, 1992), pp. 154-67.
54. Loren Ryder, 'Magnetic Sound Recording in the Motion-Picture and Television Industries', *SMPTE Journal* vol. 85, July 1976, p. 529.
55. Ibid.
56. Ibid., p. 528, figs 1 & 2.
57. Natalie Kalmus, 'Colour Consciousness', *Journal of the SMPTE* vol. 25, May 1935, pp. 145-6; Charles Handley, 'History of Motion Picture Studio Lighting', *Journal of the SMPTE* vol. 63, October 1954, reprinted in Raymond Fielding (ed.), *A Technological History of Motion Pictures and Television* (Berkeley: University of California Press, 1967), p. 123.
58. Dudley Andrews, 'The Post-War Struggle for Color', in Teresa De Laurentis and Stephen Heath (eds), *The Cinematic Apparatus* (New York, St. Martins Press, 1980), p. 69.
59. Glenn Matthews and Raife Tarkington, 'Early History of Amateur Motion-Picture Film', *Journal of SMPTE* vol. 64, March 1955, reprinted in Raymond Fielding (ed.), *A Technological History of Motion Pictures and Television* (Berkeley: University of California Press, 1967), pp. 130-168.
60. Bygrave and Goodman, 'Meet Me … ', *American Film*, October 1981, p. 42.
61. Jill Kearney, 'The Road Warrior', *American Film*, June 1988, p. 21.
62. Anon, 'Sony Does It Again in HDTV', p. 29.
63. Mokhoff, 'A Step Toward "Perfect" Resolution', p. 56.

Chapter 5: The Case of Third Dimension

1. Joseph Maria Eder, *History of Photography*, trans. by Edward Epstean (New York: Dover, 1978), p. 46.
2. James Limbacher, *Four Aspects of Film*, (New York: Brussel and Brussel, 1968), pp. 139-92.
3. Eder, *History of Photography*, p. 648.

4. David Bordwell, Janet Staiger and Kirsten Thompson, *The Classical Hollywood Cinema: Film Style and Mode of Production to 1960* (New York: Columbia University Press, 1985), p. 245.
5. Limbacher, *Four Aspects of Film*, p. 141.
6. Bordwell et al., *The Classical Hollywood Cinema*, p. 251.
7. Brian Winston, *Claiming the Real*, pp. 127–34.
8. H. J. Caufield and Sun Lu, *Applications of Holography* (New York: Wiley Interscience, 1970), pp. 23–5.
9. Dennis Gabor, 'A New Microscopic Principle', *Nature*, 161, 177 (1948).
10. Richard Gregory, *Eye & Brain*, p. 116.
11. For three centuries Newton's theory of light as corpuscles and Huygen's rival idea of light as waves through ether did battle, only to be resolved in the 20th century with the notion of quanta – packets of energy 'combining the characteristics of corpuscles and waves' (Gregory, *Eye and Brain*, p. 16).
12. Gabor's Nobel Prize for holography came in 1971.
13. Emmett Leith and Juris Upatnieks, 'Wavefront Reconstruction with Continuous-tone Objects', *Journal of the Optometric Society of America*, 54, 1295 (1964).
14. Robert Collier, Christoph Buckhard Lawrence Lin, *Optical Holography* (New York: Academic Press, 1971), pp. 21–2.
15. Ibid., pp. 418–27. As with the use of stereo-images at the beginning of the 20th century, the industrial use of holography is a rich example of post-modern confusions where the accuracy of an object, a machine-tooled part say, in the metal is tested against a holographic image of the perfect original.
16. Caulfield and Lu, *The Applications of Holography*, pp. 80–86.
17. Ibid., pp. 71–2.
18. Stewart Brand, *The Media Lab: Inventing the Future at MIT* (New York: Viking, 1987), pp. 84–7.
19. Eduardo Kac, 'Beyond the Spatial Paradigm: Time and Cinematic Form in Holographic Art', *Blimp: Zeitschrift für Film* no. 32, Autumn 1995, p. 48.
20. Collier et al., *Optical Holography*, pp. 418–26.
21. Kac, 'Beyond the Spatial Paradigm', p. 54.
22. 'Holocinema' is from Kac. The term 'Holomovie' is used by iC Holographic to describe a four-second movie hologram of Freddie Mercury. The article announcing this in *Time Out* (13–20 December 1995, p. 6) is a breathtaking example of how technological ignorance and historical amnesia feed each other: 'The hologram has come a long way since its beginning in plastic rings and naff postcards. The future of this two-dimensional sleight of eye is the Holomovie: a fully animated colour hologram capable of holding four seconds of film footage on metal foil.'
23. Kac, 'Beyond the Spatial Paradigm', p. 54. All further references to holographic movies are taken from this article, pp. 54–6.
24. Jorge Luis Börges, 'Tlön, Uqbar, Orbis Tertius', *Labyrinths: Selected Stories and Other Writings* (New York: New Directions, 1964), p. 4.

Index

141